FAVORITE BRAND NAME™

Made | Simple™

Baking

Publications International, Ltd.

Favorite Brand Name Recipes at www.fbnr.com

Photography on pages 3, 29, 33, 59, 61, 65, 71, 75, 77, 81, 89, 93, 99, 103, 109, 111, 115, 123, 127, 135, 143, 145, 149 and 153 by Proffitt Photography, Chicago.
Photographer: Laurie Proffitt
Photographer's Assistant: Chad Evans
Food Stylist: Carol Smoler
Assistant Food Stylist: Lisa Knych

Pictured on the front cover: Jo's Moist and Delicious Chocolate Cake *(page 100).*

Pictured on the back cover: Caramelized Onion Focaccia *(page 74).*

ISBN-13: 978-1-4127-2575-0
ISBN-10: 1-4127-2575-5

Library of Congress Control Number: 2007922835

Manufactured in China.

8 7 6 5 4 3 2 1

Microwave Cooking: Microwave ovens vary in wattage. Use the cooking times as guidelines and check for doneness before adding more time.

Preparation/Cooking Times: Preparation times are based on the approximate amount of time required to assemble the recipe before cooking, baking, chilling or serving. These times include preparation steps such as measuring, chopping and mixing. The fact that some preparations and cooking can be done simultaneously is taken into account. Preparation of optional ingredients and serving suggestions is not included.

irresistible
cookies

chocolate chunk cookies

2¾ cups flour
1 teaspoon baking soda
¼ teaspoon salt
¾ cup butter or margarine, softened
¾ cup firmly packed brown sugar
½ cup KARO® Light or Dark Corn Syrup
1 egg
1 teaspoon vanilla
1 package (8 ounces) semi sweet chocolate, cut into ½-inch
   chunks, divided
1 cup chopped pecans, divided

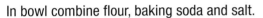

In bowl combine flour, baking soda and salt.

In mixing bowl with mixer at medium speed, beat butter and sugar until fluffy. Gradually beat in corn syrup. Beat in egg and vanilla. Gradually beat in flour mixture until just combined.

Stir in half of chocolate chunks and pecans.

Drop dough by rounded tablespoonfuls onto ungreased baking sheets. Sprinkle with remaining chocolate chunks and pecans.

Bake in 350°F oven 8 to 10 minutes or until lightly browned. Cool on wire racks.   *Makes 36 cookies*

Bake Time: 10 minutes

irresistible
cookies

pumpkin oatmeal cookies

    1 cup all-purpose flour
    1 teaspoon ground cinnamon
    ½ teaspoon salt
    ½ teaspoon ground nutmeg
    ¼ teaspoon baking soda
 1½ cups packed light brown sugar
    ½ cup (1 stick) butter, softened
    1 egg
    1 teaspoon vanilla
    ½ cup solid-pack pumpkin
    2 cups uncooked old-fashioned oats
    1 cup dried cranberries (optional)

1. Preheat oven to 350°F. Line cookie sheets with parchment paper.

2. Sift flour, cinnamon, salt, nutmeg and baking soda into medium bowl. Beat brown sugar and butter in large bowl with electric mixer at medium speed about 5 minutes or until light and fluffy.

3. Beat in egg and vanilla. Add pumpkin; beat at low speed until blended. Beat in flour mixture just until blended. Add oats; mix well. Stir in cranberries, if desired. Drop dough by heaping tablespoonfuls about 2 inches apart onto prepared cookie sheets.

4. Bake 12 minutes or until golden brown. Cool on cookie sheets 1 minute; remove to wire racks to cool completely.

Makes about 2 dozen cookies

sunshine sandwiches

⅓ cup coarse or granulated sugar
¾ cup (1½ sticks) plus 2 tablespoons butter, softened, divided
1 egg
2 tablespoons grated lemon peel
1 package (18¼ ounces) lemon cake mix with pudding in the mix
¼ cup yellow cornmeal
2 cups sifted powdered sugar
2 to 3 tablespoons lemon juice

1. Preheat oven to 375°F. Place coarse sugar in shallow bowl.

2. Beat ¾ cup butter in large bowl with electric mixer at medium speed until fluffy. Add egg and lemon peel; beat 30 seconds. Add cake mix, one third at a time, beating at low speed after each addition until combined. Stir in cornmeal. (Dough will be stiff.)

3. Shape dough into 1-inch balls; roll in sugar to coat. Place 2 inches apart on ungreased cookie sheets. Bake 8 to 9 minutes or until bottoms begin to brown. Cool on cookie sheets 1 minute; remove to wire racks to cool completely.

4. Meanwhile, beat powdered sugar and remaining 2 tablespoons butter in small bowl with electric mixer at low speed until blended. Gradually add enough lemon juice to reach spreading consistency.

5. Spread 1 slightly rounded teaspoon of frosting on bottom of one cookie. Top with second cookie, bottom side down. Repeat with remaining cookies and frosting. Store covered at room temperature for up to 24 hours or freeze.

Makes about 2 dozen sandwich cookies

sunshine sandwiches

extra chunky peanut butter cookies

    2 cups all-purpose flour
    1 teaspoon baking soda
    ½ teaspoon salt
    1 cup chunky peanut butter
    ¾ cup granulated sugar
    ½ cup packed light brown sugar
    ½ cup (1 stick) butter, softened
    2 eggs
    1 teaspoon vanilla
    1½ cups chopped chocolate-covered peanut butter cups (12 to 14 cups)
    1 cup dry roasted peanuts

1. Preheat oven to 350°F. Line cookie sheets with parchment paper or lightly grease. Combine flour, baking soda and salt in medium bowl.

2. Beat peanut butter, granulated sugar, brown sugar and butter in large bowl with electric mixer until creamy. Beat in eggs and vanilla. Add flour mixture; beat until well blended. Stir in chopped candy and peanuts.

3. Drop dough by tablespoonfuls 2 inches apart on prepared cookie sheets. Bake about 13 minutes or until set. Cool on cookie sheets 1 minute; remove to wire racks to cool completely.   *Makes about 4 dozen cookies*

jumbo 3-chip cookies

    4 cups all-purpose flour
    1 teaspoon baking powder
    1 teaspoon baking soda
    1½ cups (3 sticks) butter, softened
    1¼ cups granulated sugar
    1¼ cups packed brown sugar
    2 large eggs
    1 tablespoon vanilla extract
    1 cup (6 ounces) NESTLÉ® TOLL HOUSE® Milk Chocolate Morsels
    1 cup (6 ounces) NESTLÉ® TOLL HOUSE® Semi-Sweet Chocolate Morsels
    ½ cup NESTLÉ® TOLL HOUSE® Premier White Morsels
    1 cup chopped nuts

PREHEAT oven to 375°F.

COMBINE flour, baking powder and baking soda in medium bowl. Beat butter, granulated sugar and brown sugar in large mixer bowl until creamy. Beat in eggs and vanilla extract. Gradually beat in flour mixture. Stir in morsels and nuts. Drop dough by level ¼-cup measure 2 inches apart onto ungreased baking sheets.

BAKE for 12 to 14 minutes or until light golden brown. Cool on baking sheets for 2 minutes; remove to wire racks to cool completely. *Makes about 2 dozen cookies*

caribbean crunch shortbread

1 cup (2 sticks) butter, softened
½ cup powdered sugar
2 tablespoons packed light brown sugar
¼ teaspoon salt
2 cups all-purpose flour
1 cup diced dried tropical fruit mix, such as pineapple, mango and papaya

1. Beat butter, powdered sugar, brown sugar and salt in large bowl with electric mixer at medium speed until creamy. Add flour, ½ cup at a time, beating after each addition. Stir in dried fruit.

2. Shape dough into 14-inch log. Wrap in plastic wrap; refrigerate 1 hour.

3. Preheat oven to 300°F. Cut log into ½-inch slices; place on ungreased cookie sheets. Bake 20 to 25 minutes or until cookies are set and lightly browned. Cool on cookie sheets 5 minutes; remove to wire racks to cool completely.

Makes 28 cookies

tip | When packing cookies for gift giving, include a colorful dish towel or a decorative cloth napkin in the container—it can help cushion the cookies as well as provide an additional gift. Your choice of container can also provide a gift that lasts long after the cookies are gone. Choose decorative cookie tins, baskets or practical baking pans. Pack the cookies snugly inside to prevent breakage during transport.

carrot cake cookies

1½ cups all-purpose flour
1 teaspoon ground cinnamon
½ teaspoon baking soda
½ teaspoon salt
¾ cup packed brown sugar
½ cup (1 stick) butter, softened
1 egg
½ teaspoon vanilla
1 cup grated carrots (about 2 medium)
½ cup chopped walnuts
½ cup raisins or chopped dried pineapple (optional)

1. Preheat oven to 350°F. Grease cookie sheets or line with parchment paper. Combine flour, cinnamon, baking soda and salt in medium bowl.

2. Beat brown sugar and butter in large bowl with electric mixer at medium speed until creamy. Add egg and vanilla; beat until well blended. Stir in flour mixture; mix well. Stir in carrots, walnuts and raisins, if desired.

3. Drop dough by rounded tablespoonfuls 2 inches apart onto prepared cookie sheets. Bake 12 to 14 minutes or until set and edges are lightly browned. Cool on cookie sheets 1 minute; remove to wire racks to cool completely.

Makes about 3 dozen cookies

carrot cake cookies

mocha brownie cookies

2½ cups all-purpose flour
⅓ cup unsweetened cocoa powder
1 teaspoon baking soda
1 teaspoon baking powder
1 teaspoon salt
1 cup granulated sugar
¾ cup packed brown sugar
½ cup (1 stick) butter, softened
¼ cup sour cream
1 tablespoon instant coffee, dissolved in 2 tablespoons hot water
2 eggs
1½ cups semisweet chocolate chips

1. Preheat oven to 325°F. Combine flour, cocoa, baking soda, baking powder and salt in medium bowl.

2. Beat granulated sugar, brown sugar, butter, sour cream and coffee mixture in large bowl with electric mixer at medium speed until creamy. Add eggs, one at a time, beating well after each addition until batter is light and fluffy.

3. Gradually add flour mixture to butter mixture, beating at low speed until just blended. Beat at medium speed 1 minute or until well blended. Stir in chocolate chips.

4. Drop dough by rounded tablespoonfuls onto ungreased cookie sheets. Bake 9 to 11 minutes or until slight imprint remains when pressed with finger. Cool on cookie sheets 3 minutes; remove to wire racks to cool completely. *Makes 5 to 6 dozen cookies*

ginger polenta cookies

2¼ cups all-purpose flour
½ cup uncooked instant polenta or yellow cornmeal
½ cup toasted pistachio nuts or pine nuts, finely chopped
½ cup dried cranberries, finely chopped
   Pinch of salt
1 cup (2 sticks) butter, softened
¾ cup sugar
1 egg
1 egg yolk
½ cup finely chopped crystallized ginger
½ teaspoon ground ginger

1. Combine flour, polenta, pistachio nuts, cranberries and salt in medium bowl; mix well.

2. Beat butter and sugar in large bowl with electric mixer at medium speed until light and fluffy. Beat in egg, egg yolk, crystallized ginger and ground ginger. Add flour mixture; beat at low speed until well blended.

3. Gather dough into ball; divide in half. Shape into 2 (9-inch) logs; wrap in plastic wrap and seal ends. Roll logs to smooth surface, if necessary. Refrigerate 4 to 6 hours or until firm.

4. Preheat oven to 300°F. Line cookie sheets with parchment paper. Cut logs into ¼-inch slices; place on prepared cookie sheets. Bake 15 to 18 minutes or until edges are slightly golden. Cool on cookie sheets 2 to 3 minutes; remove to wire racks to cool completely. *Makes about 5 dozen cookies*

tip | Crystallized ginger is gingerroot that has been cooked in a sugar syrup and then coated in coarse sugar. It is typically sold in slices or chunks and is available in Asian markets and many supermarkets.

peanut butter jumbos

1½ cups peanut butter
1 cup granulated sugar
1 cup packed brown sugar
3 eggs
½ cup (1 stick) butter, softened
1 teaspoon vanilla
4½ cups uncooked old-fashioned oats
2 teaspoons baking soda
1 cup (6 ounces) semisweet chocolate chips
1 cup candy-coated chocolate pieces

1. Preheat oven to 350°F. Lightly grease cookie sheets or line with parchment paper.

2. Beat peanut butter, granulated sugar, brown sugar, eggs, butter and vanilla in large bowl with electric mixer at medium speed until well blended. Stir in oats and baking soda until well blended. Stir in chocolate chips and candy pieces.

3. Drop dough by ⅓ cupfuls 4 inches apart onto prepared cookie sheets. Press each cookie to flatten slightly. Bake 15 to 20 minutes or until firm in center. Remove to wire racks to cool completely.

Makes about 1½ dozen cookies

Peanut Butter Jumbo Sandwiches: Prepare cookies as directed. Place ⅓ cup softened chocolate or vanilla ice cream on bottom of one cookie. Top with second cookie. Lightly press sandwich together. Repeat with remaining cookies. Wrap sandwiches in plastic wrap; freeze until firm.

cut-out cookies

3½ cups all-purpose flour
2 teaspoons baking powder
¼ teaspoon salt
1 (14-ounce) can EAGLE BRAND® Sweetened Condensed Milk (NOT evaporated milk)
¾ cup (1½ sticks) butter or margarine, softened
2 eggs
1 tablespoon vanilla extract
Colored sugar sprinkles (optional)
Powdered Sugar Glaze (recipe follows, optional)

1. Combine flour, baking powder and salt. In large bowl with mixer on low speed, beat EAGLE BRAND®, butter, eggs and vanilla until just blended. Beat on medium speed 1 minute or until smooth. Add flour mixture; beat on low speed until blended. (If using hand-held mixer, use wooden spoon to add last portion of flour mixture.) Divide dough into thirds. Wrap and chill dough 2 hours or until easy to handle.

2. Preheat oven to 350°F. On lightly floured surface, roll out one portion of dough to ⅛-inch thickness. Cut out shapes. Gather dough and re-roll to use entire portion of dough. Repeat with remaining dough portions. Place cut-outs 1 inch apart on ungreased baking sheets. Sprinkle with colored sugar (optional). Bake 9 to 11 minutes or until lightly browned around edges (do not overbake). Cool 5 minutes. Remove cookies to wire racks. When cool, glaze and decorate as desired. Store covered at room temperature.   *Makes 5½ dozen cookies*

Tip: Freeze Cut-Out Cookies in a tightly sealed container.

powdered sugar glaze

2 cups sifted confectioners' sugar
½ teaspoon vanilla extract
2 tablespoons milk or whipping cream
Food coloring (optional)

Whisk powdered sugar and vanilla, adding just enough milk or cream to bind into a glaze consistency. Add food coloring (optional) to tint glaze.

cut-out cookies

cappuccino spice cookies

2½ teaspoons instant coffee granules
1 tablespoon boiling water
2⅔ cups all-purpose flour
1 teaspoon baking soda
¾ teaspoon ground cinnamon
½ teaspoon salt
¼ teaspoon ground nutmeg or ground cloves
1 cup (2 sticks) butter, softened
1 cup packed light brown sugar
½ cup granulated sugar
2 eggs
1 teaspoon vanilla
3 cups double chocolate or semisweet chocolate chips

1. Preheat oven to 375°F. Dissolve coffee in boiling water. Combine flour, baking soda, cinnamon, salt and nutmeg in medium bowl.

2. Beat butter, brown sugar and granulated sugar in large bowl with electric mixer at medium speed until light and fluffy. Add eggs, coffee and vanilla; beat until well blended. Gradually add flour mixture to butter mixture, beating at low speed until well blended. Stir in chocolate chips.

3. Drop dough by heaping tablespoonfuls 2 inches apart onto ungreased cookie sheets. Bake 8 to 10 minutes or until set. Cool on cookie sheets 1 minute; remove to wire racks to cool completely.

Makes about 3½ dozen cookies

Cappuccino Spice Minis: Prepare dough as directed above; drop by heaping teaspoonfuls onto ungreased cookie sheets. Bake 7 minutes or until set. Makes about 7 dozen mini cookies.

cappuccino spice minis

pistachio crescent cookies

2 cups all-purpose flour
2 cups finely chopped salted pistachio nuts, divided
¾ cup powdered sugar
¼ teaspoon salt
1¼ cups (2½ sticks) butter, softened, divided
½ cup mini chocolate chips
⅔ cup semisweet chocolate chips

1. Line cookie sheets with parchment paper. Combine flour, 1½ cups pistachio nuts, powdered sugar and salt in medium bowl; mix well.

2. Beat 1 cup butter in large bowl with electric mixer at medium speed until fluffy. Add flour mixture; beat until light dough forms. Beat in mini chocolate chips just until blended. Roll 1½ teaspoons dough into 2½-inch ropes; bend into crescent shapes. Arrange crescents 1 inch apart on prepared cookie sheets. Chill 30 minutes.

3. Preheat oven to 300°F. Bake cookies 10 minutes or until firm and lightly browned. Cool on cookie sheets 1 minute; remove to wire racks to cool completely.

4. For glaze, combine ⅔ cup chocolate chips and remaining ¼ cup butter in microwavable bowl. Microwave on LOW (30%) 1 minute. Stir and repeat if necessary until chocolate is melted and mixture is smooth. Place cookies on wire rack over waxed paper. Spread remaining ½ cup pistachio nuts on sheet of foil. Dip one end of each cookie in glaze, then in nuts. Let stand 30 minutes or until glaze is set.

Makes about 6 dozen cookies

chocolate truffle cookies

1 package (18 ounces) refrigerated sugar cookie dough
⅓ cup unsweetened cocoa powder
1 tablespoon powdered sugar
½ teaspoon vanilla
1 package (12 ounces) milk chocolate-covered chewy chocolate caramel candies (¾-inch squares)
¾ cup semisweet chocolate chips
    Colored sprinkles

1. Preheat oven to 325°F. Line cookie sheets with parchment paper. Place dough in large bowl; let stand at room temperature about 15 minutes.

2. Add cocoa, powdered sugar and vanilla to dough; beat with electric mixer at medium speed until well blended.

3. Shape about 2 teaspoons dough into ball; wrap ball around one caramel candy. Repeat with remaining dough and candies. Place filled balls 2 inches apart on prepared cookie sheets. Bake 12 to 15 minutes or until set. Remove to wire racks to cool completely.

4. Set wire rack over waxed paper. Place chocolate chips in small microwavable bowl. Microwave on HIGH 1 minute; stir. Microwave at additional 30-second intervals until chocolate is completely melted and smooth. Spoon small amount of chocolate over each cookie; top with sprinkles. Let stand on wire racks until set. Store in refrigerator.

Makes about 3 dozen cookies

peanut butter, oat & cherry mini cookies

½ cup granulated sugar

⅓ cup butter, softened

¼ cup packed brown sugar

¼ cup creamy peanut butter

 2 eggs

½ teaspoon vanilla

 1 cup uncooked quick-cooking oats

⅓ cup all-purpose flour

¼ cup whole wheat flour

½ teaspoon baking powder

¼ teaspoon baking soda

⅓ cup mini semisweet chocolate chips

¼ cup dried cherries, coarsely chopped

1. Preheat oven to 375°F.

2. Beat granulated sugar, butter, brown sugar and peanut butter in large bowl with electric mixer at medium speed until creamy. Add eggs and vanilla; beat until well blended. Add oats, flours, baking powder and baking soda; beat at low speed until blended. Stir in chocolate chips and cherries.

3. Drop mixture by slightly rounded teaspoonfuls onto ungreased cookie sheets. Bake 8 to 9 minutes or until light brown. Cool on cookie sheets 1 minute; remove to wire racks to cool completely.

Makes 8 dozen mini cookies

Prep Time: 10 minutes
Bake Time: 8 minutes

brownies & bars

mocha fudge brownies

   3 **squares (1 ounce each) semisweet chocolate**
¾ **cup sugar**
½ **cup (1 stick) butter, softened**
   2 **eggs**
   2 **teaspoons instant espresso powder**
   1 **teaspoon vanilla**
½ **cup all-purpose flour**
½ **cup chopped toasted almonds**
   1 **cup (6 ounces) milk chocolate chips, divided**

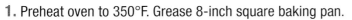

1. Preheat oven to 350°F. Grease 8-inch square baking pan.

2. Melt semisweet chocolate in top of double boiler over hot, not boiling, water. Remove from heat; let cool slightly.

3. Beat sugar and butter in medium bowl with electric mixer at medium speed until well blended. Add eggs; beat until light and fluffy. Add melted chocolate, espresso powder and vanilla; beat until well blended. Stir in flour, almonds and ½ cup chocolate chips. Spread batter evenly in prepared pan.

4. Bake 25 minutes or just until firm in center. Remove from oven; sprinkle with remaining ½ cup chocolate chips. Let stand until chips melt; spread chocolate evenly over brownies. Cool completely in pan on wire rack. Cut into 2-inch squares.
Makes 16 brownies

brownies
& bars

cranberry coconut bars

Filling
>   **2 cups fresh or frozen cranberries**
>   **1 cup dried sweetened cranberries**
>   **⅔ cup granulated sugar**
>   **¼ cup water**
>   **Peel of 1 lemon**

Crust
>   **1¼ cups all-purpose flour**
>   **¾ cup uncooked old-fashioned oats**
>   **½ teaspoon baking soda**
>   **½ teaspoon salt**
>   **¾ cup (1½ sticks) butter, softened**
>   **1 cup firmly packed light brown sugar**
>   **1 cup chopped toasted pecans***
>   **1 cup shredded sweetened coconut**

*To toast pecans, spread in single layer on baking sheet. Bake in preheated 350°F oven 5 to 7 minutes or until golden brown, stirring frequently.

1. Preheat oven to 400°F. Grease and flour 13×9-inch baking pan.

2. For filling, combine fresh cranberries, dried cranberries, granulated sugar, water and lemon peel in medium saucepan. Cook 10 to 15 minutes over medium-high heat until mixture is pulpy, stirring frequently. Mash cranberries with back of spoon. Cool to lukewarm.

3. For crust, combine flour, oats, baking soda and salt in medium bowl. Beat butter and brown sugar in large bowl with electric mixer until creamy. Add flour mixture; beat just until blended. Stir in pecans and coconut. Reserve 1½ cups; pat remaining mixture onto bottom of prepared pan. Bake 10 minutes; remove from oven.

4. Gently spread cranberry filling over crust; sprinkle with reserved crumb mixture. Bake 18 to 20 minutes or until set and crust is golden brown. Cool completely before cutting into bars.   *Makes 2 dozen bars*

Note: You can make these bars when fresh or frozen cranberries aren't available. Prepare the filling using 2 cups dried sweetened cranberries, 1 cup water and peel of 1 lemon; cook 8 to 10 minutes over medium heat, stirring frequently. Use as directed in step 4.

o'henrietta bars

MAZOLA NO STICK® Cooking Spray
½ **cup (1 stick) margarine or butter, softened**
½ **cup packed brown sugar**
½ **cup KARO® Light or Dark Corn Syrup**
1 **teaspoon vanilla**
3 **cups quick oats, uncooked**
½ **cup (3 ounces) semisweet chocolate chips**
¼ **cup creamy peanut butter**

1. Preheat oven to 350°F. Spray 8- or 9-inch square baking pan with cooking spray.

2. In large bowl with mixer at medium speed, beat margarine, brown sugar, corn syrup and vanilla until smooth. Stir in oats. Press into prepared pan.

3. Bake 25 minutes or until center is barely firm. Cool on wire rack 5 minutes.

4. Sprinkle with chocolate chips; top with small spoonfuls of peanut butter. Let stand 5 minutes; spread peanut butter and chocolate over bars, swirling to marbleize.

5. Cool completely on wire rack before cutting. Cut into bars; refrigerate 15 minutes to set topping.

Makes 24 bars

Prep Time: 20 minutes
Bake Time: 25 minutes, plus cooling

chunky caramel nut brownies

¾ cup (1½ sticks) butter
4 squares (1 ounce each) unsweetened chocolate
2 cups sugar
4 eggs
1 cup all-purpose flour
1 package (14 ounces) caramels
¼ cup whipping cream
2 cups pecan halves or coarsely chopped pecans, divided
1 package (12 ounces) chocolate chunks or chips

1. Preheat oven to 350°F. Grease 13×9-inch baking pan.

2. Place butter and chocolate in large microwavable bowl. Microwave on HIGH 1½ to 2 minutes or until chocolate is melted and mixture is smooth when stirred. Stir in sugar until well blended. Beat in eggs, one at a time. Stir in flour until well blended. Spread half of batter in prepared pan. Bake 20 minutes.

3. Meanwhile, combine caramels and cream in medium microwavable bowl. Microwave on HIGH 1½ to 2 minutes or until caramels begin to melt; stir until mixture is smooth. Stir in 1 cup pecan halves.

4. Spread caramel mixture over partially baked brownie base. Sprinkle with half of chocolate chunks. Pour remaining brownie batter over top; sprinkle with remaining 1 cup pecan halves and chocolate chunks. Bake 25 to 30 minutes or until set. Cool completely in pan on wire rack. Cut into squares.

Makes 2 dozen brownies

marbled cheesecake bars

Chocolate Crust (recipe follows)
3 packages (8 ounces each) cream cheese, softened
1 can (14 ounces) sweetened condensed milk (not evaporated milk)
3 eggs
2 teaspoons vanilla extract
4 sections (½ ounce each) HERSHEY'S Unsweetened Baking Chocolate, melted

1. Prepare Chocolate Crust. Heat oven to 300°F.

2. Beat cream cheese in large bowl until fluffy. Gradually add sweetened condensed milk, beating until smooth. Add eggs and vanilla; mix well.

3. Pour half of batter evenly over prepared crust. Stir melted chocolate into remaining batter; drop by teaspoons over vanilla batter. With metal spatula or knife, swirl gently through batter to marble.

4. Bake 45 to 50 minutes or until set. Cool in pan on wire rack. Refrigerate several hours until chilled. Cut into bars. Cover; store leftover bars in refrigerator.   *Makes 24 to 36 bars*

Chocolate Crust: Stir together 2 cups vanilla wafer crumbs (about 60 wafers), ⅓ cup HERSHEY'S Cocoa and ½ cup powdered sugar. Stir in ½ cup (1 stick) melted butter or margarine until well blended. Press mixture firmly into bottom of ungreased 13×9×2-inch baking pan.

Prep Time: 25 minutes
Bake Time: 45 minutes
Cool Time: 1 hour
Chill Time: 2½ hours

marbled cheesecake bar

peanut butter cookie bars

1 package (18 ounces) refrigerated peanut butter cookie dough
1 can (14 ounces) sweetened condensed milk
¼ cup all-purpose flour
¼ cup peanut butter
1 cup peanut butter chips
1 cup chopped peanuts

1. Preheat oven to 350°F. Lightly grease 13×9-inch baking pan. Let dough stand at room temperature about 15 minutes.

2. Press dough evenly onto bottom of prepared pan. Bake 10 minutes.

3. Meanwhile, combine sweetened condensed milk, flour and peanut butter in medium bowl; beat with electric mixer at medium speed until well blended. Spoon over partially baked crust. Sprinkle evenly with peanut butter chips and peanuts; press down lightly.

4. Bake 15 to 18 minutes or until center is set. Cool completely in pan on wire rack.

Makes 2 dozen bars

tip | These simple bar cookies are very easy to dress up with a drizzle of chocolate. Melt 1 cup chips (milk, semisweet and/or white chocolate) in the microwave according to package directions, then drizzle over the bars with a fork. Let the glaze set before cutting into bars.

intense mint-chocolate brownies

Brownies

    1 cup (2 sticks) butter

    4 squares (1 ounce each) unsweetened chocolate

  1½ cups granulated sugar

    3 eggs

    ½ teaspoon salt

    ½ teaspoon mint extract

    ½ teaspoon vanilla

    ¾ cup all-purpose flour

Mint Frosting

    6 tablespoons butter, softened

    1 teaspoon mint extract

    2 to 3 drops green food coloring

    2 cups powdered sugar

    2 to 3 tablespoons milk

Chocolate Glaze

    ⅓ cup semisweet chocolate chips

    2 tablespoons butter

1. Preheat oven to 325°F. Grease and flour 9-inch square baking pan.

2. For brownies, melt butter and chocolate in top of double boiler over simmering water. Beat chocolate mixture, granulated sugar, eggs, mint extract, vanilla and salt in large bowl until well blended. Stir in flour. Spread batter in prepared pan. Bake 35 minutes or until top is firm and edges begin to pull away from sides of pan. Cool completely in pan on wire rack.

3. For frosting, beat butter, mint extract and food coloring in large bowl with electric mixer at medium speed until fluffy. Add powdered sugar, ½ cup at a time, beating well after each addition. Beat in milk, 1 tablespoon at a time, until of spreading consistency. Spread frosting over cooled brownies.

4. For chocolate glaze, place chocolate chips and butter in microwavable bowl. Microwave on LOW (30%) 1 minute; stir. Repeat until chocolate chips are melted and mixture is smooth. Drizzle glaze over frosting. Let stand 30 minutes or until glaze is set.

Makes 2 dozen brownies

lemony cheesecake bars

1½ cups graham cracker crumbs
⅓ cup sugar
⅓ cup finely chopped pecans
⅓ cup (⅔ stick) butter or margarine, melted
2 (8-ounce) packages cream cheese, softened
1 (14-ounce) can EAGLE BRAND® Sweetened Condensed Milk (NOT evaporated milk)
2 eggs
½ cup lemon juice

1. Preheat oven to 325°F. In medium bowl, combine graham cracker crumbs, sugar, pecans and butter. Reserve ⅓ cup crumb mixture; press remaining mixture firmly on bottom of ungreased 13×9-inch baking pan. Bake 5 minutes. Cool on wire rack.

2. In large bowl, beat cream cheese until fluffy. Gradually beat in EAGLE BRAND® until smooth. Add eggs; beat until just blended. Stir in lemon juice. Carefully spoon mixture on top of crust. Spoon reserved crumb mixture to make diagonal stripes on top of cream cheese mixture or sprinkle to cover.

3. Bake about 30 minutes or until knife inserted near center comes out clean. Cool on wire rack 1 hour. Chill in refrigerator until serving time. Cut into bars. Store leftovers covered in refrigerator.   *Makes 2 dozen bars*

Prep Time: 25 minutes
Bake Time: 35 minutes
Cool Time: 1 hour

mississippi mud bars

¾ **cup packed brown sugar**
½ **cup (1 stick) butter, softened**
 1 **egg**
 1 **teaspoon vanilla**
½ **teaspoon baking soda**
¼ **teaspoon salt**
 1 **cup plus 2 tablespoons all-purpose flour**
 1 **cup (6 ounces) semisweet chocolate chips, divided**
 1 **cup (6 ounces) white chocolate chips, divided**
½ **cup chopped walnuts or pecans**

1. Preheat oven to 375°F. Line 9-inch square pan with foil; grease foil.

2. Beat brown sugar and butter in large bowl with electric mixer at medium speed until well blended. Beat in egg and vanilla until light. Blend in baking soda and salt. Add flour, mixing until well blended. Stir in ⅔ cup semisweet chips, ⅔ cup white chips and nuts. Spread dough in prepared pan.

3. Bake 23 to 25 minutes or until center feels firm. *Do not overbake.* Remove from oven; sprinkle with remaining ⅓ cup semisweet chips and ⅓ cup white chips. Let stand until chips melt; spread evenly over bars. Cool in pan on wire rack until chocolate is set. Cut into bars or triangles.   *Makes about 3 dozen bars or triangles*

chocolatey raspberry crumb bars

1 cup (2 sticks) butter or margarine, softened
2 cups all-purpose flour
½ cup packed light brown sugar
¼ teaspoon salt
2 cups (12-ounce package) NESTLÉ® TOLL HOUSE® Semi-Sweet Chocolate Morsels, *divided*
1 can (14 ounces) NESTLÉ® CARNATION® Sweetened Condensed Milk
½ cup chopped nuts (optional)
⅓ cup seedless raspberry jam

PREHEAT oven to 350°F. Grease 13×9-inch baking pan.

BEAT butter in large mixer bowl until creamy. Beat in flour, sugar and salt until crumbly. With floured fingers, press *1¾ cups* crumb mixture onto bottom of prepared baking pan; reserve *remaining* mixture.

BAKE for 10 to 12 minutes or until edges are golden brown.

MICROWAVE *1 cup* morsels and sweetened condensed milk in medium, uncovered, microwave-safe bowl on HIGH (100%) power for 1 minute. STIR. Morsels may retain some of their original shape. If necessary, microwave at additional 10- to 15-second intervals, stirring just until morsels are melted. Spread over hot crust.

STIR nuts into *reserved* crumb mixture; sprinkle over chocolate layer. Drop teaspoonfuls of raspberry jam over crumb mixture. Sprinkle with *remaining* morsels.

BAKE for 25 to 30 minutes or until center is set. Cool in pan on wire rack. Cut into bars.

Makes 3 dozen bars

tangy lime bars

1 package (18 ounces) refrigerated sugar cookie dough
¾ cup all-purpose flour, divided
1¼ cups granulated sugar
4 eggs
½ cup bottled key lime juice
1 drop green food coloring
1 teaspoon baking powder
Powdered sugar

1. Preheat oven to 350°F. Lightly grease 13×9-inch baking pan. Let dough stand at room temperature about 15 minutes.

2. Beat dough and ½ cup flour in large bowl until well blended. Press dough evenly onto bottom and ½ inch up sides of prepared pan. Bake 20 minutes.

3. Meanwhile, beat granulated sugar, eggs, lime juice and food coloring in large bowl with electric mixer at medium speed until well blended. Add remaining ¼ cup flour and baking powder; beat until well blended. Pour over baked crust.

4. Bake 18 to 21 minutes or until edges are brown and center is just set. Cool completely in pan on wire rack. Sprinkle with powdered sugar just before serving. Store leftovers covered in refrigerator.

Makes 2 dozen bars

rocky road brownies

1¼ cups miniature marshmallows
1 cup HERSHEY'S Semi-Sweet Chocolate Chips
½ cup chopped nuts
½ cup (1 stick) butter or margarine
1 cup sugar
2 eggs
1 teaspoon vanilla extract
½ cup all-purpose flour
⅓ cup HERSHEY'S Cocoa
½ teaspoon baking powder
½ teaspoon salt

1. Heat oven to 350°F. Grease 9-inch square baking pan.

2. Stir together marshmallows, chocolate chips and nuts; set aside. Place butter in large microwave-safe bowl. Microwave at HIGH (100%) 1 to 1½ minutes or until melted. Add sugar, eggs and vanilla, beating with spoon until well blended. Add flour, cocoa, baking powder and salt; blend well. Spread batter in prepared pan.

3. Bake 22 minutes. Sprinkle chocolate chip mixture over top. Continue baking 5 minutes or until marshmallows have softened and puffed slightly. Cool completely. With wet knife, cut into squares.

Makes about 20 brownies

rocky road brownies

banana oatmeal snack bars

2 packages (18 ounces each) refrigerated oatmeal raisin cookie dough
2 bananas, mashed
3 eggs
½ teaspoon ground cinnamon
1 cup uncooked old-fashioned oats
1 cup dried cranberries
½ cup chopped dried apricots
½ cup chopped pecans
  Powdered sugar

1. Preheat oven to 350°F. Lightly grease 13×9-inch baking pan. Let dough stand at room temperature about 15 minutes.

2. Beat cookie dough, bananas, eggs and cinnamon in large bowl until well blended. Combine oats, cranberries, apricots and pecans in medium bowl; stir into dough until well blended. Spread in prepared pan; smooth top.

3. Bake 40 to 45 minutes or until top is brown and toothpick inserted into center comes out clean. Cool completely in pan on wire rack. Sprinkle with powdered sugar just before serving. *Makes 2 dozen bars*

chewy peanut butter brownies

¾ cup (1½ sticks) butter, melted
¾ cup creamy peanut butter
1¾ cups sugar
2 teaspoons vanilla
4 eggs, lightly beaten
1¼ cups all-purpose flour
½ teaspoon baking powder
¼ teaspoon salt
¼ cup unsweetened cocoa powder

1. Preheat oven to 350°F. Grease 13×9-inch baking pan.

2. Beat butter and peanut butter in large bowl until well blended. Add sugar and vanilla; beat until blended. Add eggs; beat until well blended. Stir in flour, baking powder and salt just until blended. Reserve 1¾ cups batter. Stir cocoa into remaining batter.

3. Spread cocoa batter evenly in prepared pan. Top with reserved batter. Bake 30 minutes or until edges begin to pull away from sides of pan. Cool completely in pan on wire rack. *Makes 3 dozen brownies*

tip | Stored in an airtight container in a cool, dark place, cocoa powder can last for up to 2 years. (The color may lighten somewhat, but the flavor will still be good.) If you are using cocoa that has been in your pantry for a while, sift it before adding it to the batter.

piña colada cookie bars

½ cup (1 stick) butter, melted
1½ cups graham cracker crumbs
1 can (14 ounces) sweetened condensed milk
2 tablespoons dark rum
2 cups white chocolate chips
1 cup flaked coconut
½ cup chopped macadamia nuts
½ cup chopped dried pineapple

1. Preheat oven to 350°F.

2. Pour butter into 13×9-inch baking pan, tilting pan to coat bottom. Sprinkle graham cracker crumbs evenly over butter. Blend sweetened condensed milk and rum in small bowl; pour over crumbs. Top with white chips, coconut, nuts and pineapple.

3. Bake 25 to 30 minutes or until edges are lightly browned. Cut into bars with serrated knife. Store loosely covered at room temperature.

Makes 3 dozen bars

chunky pecan pie bars

Crust
- 1½ cups all-purpose flour
- ½ cup (1 stick) butter or margarine, softened
- ¼ cup packed brown sugar

Filling
- 3 large eggs
- ¾ cup corn syrup
- ¾ cup granulated sugar
- 2 tablespoons butter or margarine, melted
- 1 teaspoon vanilla extract
- 1¾ cups (11.5-ounce package) NESTLÉ® TOLL HOUSE® Semi-Sweet Chocolate Chunks
- 1½ cups coarsely chopped pecans

PREHEAT oven to 350°F. Grease 13×9-inch baking pan.

For Crust

BEAT flour, butter and brown sugar in small mixer bowl until crumbly. Press into prepared baking pan.

BAKE for 12 to 15 minutes or until lightly browned.

For Filling

BEAT eggs, corn syrup, granulated sugar, butter and vanilla extract in medium bowl with wire whisk. Stir in chunks and nuts. Pour evenly over baked crust.

BAKE for 25 to 30 minutes or until set. Cool completely in pan on wire rack. Cut into bars.

Makes 2 to 3 dozen bars

breads
& muffins

prosciutto provolone rolls

1 loaf (1 pound) frozen bread dough, thawed
¼ cup garlic and herb spreadable cheese
6 thin slices prosciutto (about one 3-ounce package) or deli ham
6 slices (1 ounce each) provolone cheese

1. Spray 12 standard (2¾-inch) muffin pan cups with nonstick cooking spray. Roll out dough on lightly floured surface to 12×10-inch rectangle.

2. Spread garlic and herb cheese evenly over dough. Arrange prosciutto slices over cheese; top with provolone slices. Starting with long side, roll up dough jelly-roll style; pinch seam to seal.

3. Cut crosswise into 1-inch slices; arrange slices cut sides down in prepared muffin cups. Cover and let rise in warm, draft-free place 30 to 40 minutes or until nearly doubled in bulk. Preheat oven to 350°F.

4. Bake rolls about 18 minutes or until golden brown. Loosen edges of rolls with knife; remove from pan to wire rack. Serve warm.

Makes 12 rolls

breads
& muffins

fiesta corn bread

2 cups all-purpose flour
1½ cups white or yellow cornmeal
1½ cups (6 ounces) shredded Cheddar cheese
1 can (7 ounces) ORTEGA® Diced Green Chiles
½ cup granulated sugar
1 tablespoon baking powder
1½ teaspoons salt
1 can (12 fluid ounces) CARNATION® Evaporated Milk
½ cup vegetable oil
2 large eggs, lightly beaten

PREHEAT oven to 375°F. Grease 13×9-inch baking pan.

COMBINE flour, cornmeal, cheese, chiles, sugar, baking powder and salt in large bowl; mix well. Add evaporated milk, vegetable oil and eggs; stir just until moistened. Spread in prepared baking pan.

BAKE for 30 to 35 minutes or until wooden pick inserted in center comes out clean. Cool in pan on wire rack for 10 minutes; cut into squares. Serve warm. *Makes 12 servings*

jumbo streusel-topped raspberry muffins

2¼ cups all-purpose flour, divided
¼ cup packed brown sugar
2 tablespoons butter
¾ cup granulated sugar
2 teaspoons baking powder
½ teaspoon baking soda
½ teaspoon salt
½ teaspoon grated lemon peel
¾ cup plus 2 tablespoons milk
⅓ cup butter, melted
1 egg, beaten
2 cups fresh or frozen raspberries (do not thaw)

1. Preheat oven to 350°F. Grease 6 jumbo (3½-inch) muffin pan cups.

2. For topping, combine ¼ cup flour and brown sugar in small bowl. Cut in 2 tablespoons butter with pastry blender or two knives until mixture forms coarse crumbs.

3. Reserve ¼ cup flour; set aside. Combine remaining 1¾ cups flour, granulated sugar, baking powder, baking soda, salt and lemon peel in medium bowl. Combine milk, melted butter and egg in small bowl.

4. Add milk mixture to flour mixture; stir until almost blended. Toss frozen raspberries with reserved flour in medium bowl just until coated; gently fold raspberries into muffin batter. Spoon batter into prepared muffin cups, filling three-fourths full. Sprinkle with topping.

5. Bake 25 to 30 minutes or until toothpick inserted into centers comes out clean. Cool in pan 2 minutes; remove to wire rack. Serve warm or at room temperature. *Makes 6 jumbo muffins*

Variation: For regular-size muffins, spoon batter into 12 standard (2½-inch) greased or paper-lined muffin cups. Bake at 350°F 21 to 24 minutes or until toothpick inserted into centers comes out clean. Makes 12 muffins.

jumbo streusel-topped
raspberry muffins

pesto-parmesan twists

1 loaf (1 pound) frozen bread dough, thawed
¼ cup prepared pesto sauce
⅔ cup grated Parmesan cheese, divided
1 tablespoon olive oil

1. Line baking sheets with parchment paper. Roll out dough to 20×10-inch rectangle on lightly floured surface.

2. Spread pesto evenly over half of dough; sprinkle with ⅓ cup Parmesan. Fold remaining half of dough over filling, forming 10-inch square. Roll square into 12×10-inch rectangle. Cut into 12 (1-inch) strips with sharp knife. Cut strips in half crosswise to form 24 strips total.

3. Twist each strip several times; place on prepared baking sheets. Cover and let rise in warm, draft-free place 20 minutes.

4. Preheat oven to 350°F. Brush breadsticks with oil; sprinkle with remaining ⅓ cup Parmesan. Bake 16 to 18 minutes or until golden brown.   *Makes 2 dozen breadsticks*

irish soda bread rounds

4 cups all-purpose flour
¼ cup sugar
1 tablespoon baking powder
1 teaspoon baking soda
1 teaspoon salt
⅓ cup shortening
1 cup currants or raisins
1¾ cups buttermilk
1 egg

1. Preheat oven to 350°F. Grease 2 baking sheets.

2. Sift flour, sugar, baking powder, baking soda and salt into large bowl. Cut in shortening with pastry blender or two knives until mixture resembles coarse crumbs. Stir in currants. Beat buttermilk and egg in medium bowl until well blended. Add buttermilk mixture to flour mixture; stir until mixture forms soft dough that clings together and forms a ball.

3. Turn out dough onto well-floured surface. Knead dough gently 10 to 12 times. Shape dough into 8 (3½-inch) rounds; place rounds on prepared baking sheets. Score top of each round with tip of sharp knife, making an "X" about 1 inch long and ¼ inch deep.

4. Bake 25 to 28 minutes or until toothpick inserted into centers comes out clean. Immediately remove from baking sheets; cool on wire racks.*

Makes 8 rounds

*For a sweet crust, combine 1 tablespoon sugar and 1 tablespoon water in small bowl; brush over hot bread.

apricot mini muffins

1½ cups all-purpose flour
½ cup sugar
½ cup finely chopped dried apricots
¼ teaspoon baking powder
¼ teaspoon baking soda
⅛ teaspoon salt
  Pinch ground nutmeg
½ cup (1 stick) butter, melted and cooled to room temperature
2 eggs
2 tablespoons milk
1 teaspoon vanilla

1. Preheat oven to 350°F. Spray 24 mini (1¾-inch) muffin pan cups with nonstick cooking spray.

2. Combine flour, sugar, apricots, baking powder, baking soda, salt and nutmeg in large bowl; mix well. Whisk butter, eggs, milk and vanilla in medium bowl. Add butter mixture to flour mixture; mix just until blended. Spoon about 1 tablespoon batter into each prepared muffin cup.

3. Bake 12 to 15 minutes or until toothpick inserted into centers comes out clean.

Makes 2 dozen mini muffins

savory cheddar bread

2 cups all-purpose flour
4 teaspoons baking powder
1 tablespoon sugar
½ teaspoon onion salt
½ teaspoon oregano, crushed
¼ teaspoon dry mustard
1 cup (4 ounces) SARGENTO® Fancy Mild or Sharp Cheddar Shredded Cheese
1 cup milk
1 egg, beaten
1 tablespoon butter or margarine, melted

In large bowl, stir together flour, baking powder, sugar, onion salt, oregano, dry mustard and cheese. In separate bowl, combine milk, egg and melted butter; add to dry ingredients, stirring just until moistened. Spread batter in greased 8×4-inch loaf pan. Bake at 350°F 45 minutes or until wooden pick inserted in center comes out clean. Cool 10 minutes on wire rack. Remove from pan. *Makes 16 slices*

tip | Dry mustard is the powder that results from grinding mustard seeds; it can be found with other spices in the supermarket. Dry mustard is a strong flavor, so recipes often call for only small amounts. Purchase a small jar if possible, as dry mustard can be stored in a cool, dark place for up to 6 months.

mixed-up muffins

2 cups all-purpose flour
1 cup sugar, divided
2 teaspoons baking powder
½ teaspoon baking soda
¼ teaspoon salt
⅓ cup mini chocolate chips
⅓ cup unsweetened cocoa powder
1¼ cups milk
2 eggs
⅓ cup vegetable oil
1 teaspoon vanilla

1. Preheat oven to 400°F. Line 15 standard (2½-inch) muffin pan cups with paper baking cups or spray with nonstick cooking spray.

2. Combine flour, ¾ cup sugar, baking powder, baking soda and salt in medium bowl. Remove 1½ cups mixture to another bowl; stir in chocolate chips. Stir cocoa and remaining ¼ cup sugar into remaining flour mixture.

3. Beat milk, eggs, oil and vanilla in large glass measuring cup or medium bowl. Add half of milk mixture to each bowl of dry ingredients. Stir each batter separately just until blended. Spoon white and chocolate batters side by side into each muffin cup, filling about three-fourths full.

4. Bake 20 to 25 minutes or until toothpick inserted into centers comes out clean. Cool in pans 2 minutes; remove to wire racks. Serve warm or at room temperature. *Makes 15 muffins*

caramelized onion focaccia

2 tablespoons plus 1 teaspoon olive oil, divided
4 medium onions, cut in half and thinly sliced
½ teaspoon salt
2 tablespoons water
1 tablespoon chopped fresh rosemary
¼ teaspoon ground black pepper
1 loaf (1 pound) frozen bread dough, thawed
1 cup (4 ounces) shredded fontina cheese
¼ cup grated Parmesan cheese

1. Heat 2 tablespoons oil in large skillet over high heat. Add onions and salt; cook about 10 minutes or until onions begin to brown, stirring occasionally. Stir in water. Reduce heat to medium; partially cover and cook about 20 minutes or until onions are deep golden brown, stirring occasionally. Remove from heat; stir in rosemary and pepper. Let cool slightly.

2. Meanwhile, brush 13×9-inch baking pan with remaining 1 teaspoon oil. Roll out dough to 13×9-inch rectangle on lightly floured surface. Transfer dough to prepared pan; cover and let rise in warm, draft-free place 30 minutes.

3. Preheat oven to 375°F. Prick dough all over (about 12 times) with fork. Sprinkle fontina over dough; top with caramelized onions. Sprinkle with Parmesan.

4. Bake 18 to 20 minutes or until golden brown. Remove from pan to wire rack. Cut into squares; serve warm.

Makes 12 servings

orange cinnamon rolls

½ **cup packed brown sugar**
3 **tablespoons butter, melted, divided**
1 **tablespoon ground cinnamon**
1 **teaspoon grated orange peel**
1 **loaf (1 pound) frozen bread dough, thawed**
⅓ **cup raisins (optional)**
½ **cup powdered sugar, sifted**
1 **to 2 tablespoons fresh orange juice**

1. Grease 2 (8-inch) round cake pans. Combine brown sugar, 1 tablespoon butter, cinnamon and orange peel in small bowl; mix well.

2. Roll out dough on lightly floured surface to 18×8-inch rectangle. Brush dough with remaining 2 tablespoons butter; spread evenly with brown sugar mixture. Sprinkle with raisins, if desired. Starting with long side, roll up dough jelly-roll style; pinch seam to seal. Cut crosswise into 1-inch slices; arrange slices cut sides down in prepared pans. Cover and let rise in warm, draft-free place 30 to 40 minutes or until nearly doubled in bulk.

3. Preheat oven to 350°F. Bake rolls about 18 minutes or until light golden brown. Immediately remove rolls from pan to wire rack to cool slightly.

4. Blend powdered sugar and orange juice in small bowl until smooth and consistency is thin enough to pour. Drizzle glaze over warm rolls.

Makes 18 cinnamon rolls

bacon cheddar muffins

  2 cups all-purpose flour
¾ cup sugar
  2 teaspoons baking powder
½ teaspoon baking soda
½ teaspoon salt
¾ cup plus 2 tablespoons milk
⅓ cup butter, melted
  1 egg, lightly beaten
  1 cup (4 ounces) shredded Cheddar cheese
½ cup crumbled crisp-cooked bacon (about 6 slices)

1. Preheat oven to 350°F. Grease 12 standard (2½-inch) muffin pan cups or line with paper baking cups.

2. Combine flour, sugar, baking powder, baking soda and salt in medium bowl. Combine milk, butter and egg in small bowl; mix well. Add milk mixture to flour mixture; stir just until blended. Gently stir in cheese and bacon. Spoon batter evenly into prepared muffin cups, filling three-fourths full.

3. Bake 15 to 20 minutes or until toothpick inserted into centers comes out clean. Cool in pan 2 minutes; remove to wire rack. Serve warm or at room temperature. *Makes 12 muffins*

ham & swiss cheese biscuits

  2 cups all-purpose flour
  2 teaspoons baking powder
½ teaspoon baking soda
½ cup (1 stick) butter, chilled and cut into pieces
½ cup (2 ounces) shredded Swiss cheese
  2 ounces ham, minced
⅔ cup buttermilk

1. Preheat oven to 450°F. Grease baking sheet. Sift flour, baking powder and baking soda into medium bowl. Cut in butter with pastry blender or two knives until mixture resembles coarse crumbs. Stir in cheese, ham and enough buttermilk to make soft dough.

2. Turn out dough onto lightly floured surface; knead lightly. Roll out dough ½ inch thick. Cut out biscuits with 2-inch round cutter. Place on prepared baking sheet.

3. Bake about 10 minutes or until browned. *Makes about 18 biscuits*

sweet potato muffins

    2 cups all-purpose flour
    ¾ cup chopped walnuts
    ¾ cup golden raisins
    ½ cup packed brown sugar
    1 tablespoon baking powder
    1 teaspoon ground cinnamon
    ½ teaspoon baking soda
    ½ teaspoon salt
    ¼ teaspoon ground nutmeg
    1 cup mashed cooked sweet potato
    ¾ cup milk
    ½ cup (1 stick) butter, melted
    2 eggs, beaten
 1½ teaspoons vanilla

1. Preheat oven to 400°F. Grease 24 standard (2½-inch) muffin pan cups.

2. Combine flour, walnuts, raisins, brown sugar, baking powder, cinnamon, baking soda, salt and nutmeg in medium bowl; stir until well blended. Combine sweet potato, milk, butter, eggs and vanilla in large bowl; mix well. Add flour mixture; stir just until ingredients are moistened. Spoon batter evenly into prepared muffin cups.

3. Bake 15 minutes or until toothpick inserted into centers comes out clean. Cool in pans 5 minutes; remove to wire racks to cool. *Makes 24 muffins*

southwestern sausage drop biscuits

   1 pound BOB EVANS® Zesty Hot Roll Sausage
   3 cups all-purpose (biscuit) baking mix
1¼ cups (5 ounces) shredded sharp Cheddar cheese
   1 cup seeded diced fresh or drained canned tomatoes
   1 cup chopped green onions
   1 cup milk
   ¼ teaspoon paprika
    Dash cayenne pepper
    Butter (optional)

Preheat oven to 350°F. Crumble and cook sausage in medium skillet until browned. Drain on paper towels. Combine sausage and remaining ingredients except butter in large bowl; mix well. Shape dough into 2-inch balls; place on ungreased baking sheet. Bake 12 minutes or until golden. Serve hot with butter, if desired. Refrigerate leftovers.

Makes about 2 dozen small biscuits

tip | In the middle of winter (or any other time good ripe tomatoes are hard to find), canned tomatoes make an excellent substitute for fresh. There are plenty of good-quality canned tomato products available, and they always have much more flavor than out-of-season or underripe tomatoes.

hot cross buns

1 package (¼ ounce) active dry yeast
1 cup warm milk, divided
2¼ cups all-purpose flour
½ cup whole wheat flour
1 cup currants
¼ cup granulated sugar
¼ teaspoon salt
¼ teaspoon ground nutmeg
2 eggs, beaten
¼ cup (½ stick) butter, melted
½ cup powdered sugar
1 to 2 tablespoons milk or cream

1. Sprinkle yeast over ¼ cup warm milk in small bowl; stir to dissolve yeast. Let stand 10 minutes or until bubbly. Meanwhile, combine flours, currants, granulated sugar, salt and nutmeg in medium bowl. Blend eggs, butter and remaining ¾ cup warm milk in large bowl.

2. Stir dissolved yeast into egg mixture. Gradually beat in flour mixture until well blended. (Dough will be sticky.) Cover and let rise in warm place 1 hour.

3. Preheat oven to 400°F. Grease 12 standard (2½-inch) muffin pan cups. Vigorously stir down dough with wooden spoon. Spoon about ¼ cup dough into each muffin cup; smooth tops.

4. Bake 20 minutes or until golden brown. Cool buns in pan on wire rack 5 minutes; remove to wire rack to cool completely.

5. For icing, blend powdered sugar and milk in small bowl until smooth. Spoon into small resealable food storage bag. Cut off tiny corner of bag; pipe cross on center of each bun.   *Makes 12 buns*

lots o' chocolate bread

        2 cups mini semisweet chocolate chips, divided
    ⅔ cup packed light brown sugar
    ½ cup (1 stick) butter, softened
        2 eggs
    2½ cups all-purpose flour
    1½ cups applesauce
    1½ teaspoons vanilla
        1 teaspoon baking soda
        1 teaspoon baking powder
    ½ teaspoon salt
        1 tablespoon shortening (do not use butter, margarine, spread or oil)

1. Preheat oven to 350°F. Grease 5 mini (5½×3-inch) loaf pans. Place 1 cup chocolate chips in small microwavable bowl. Microwave on HIGH 1 minute; stir. Microwave at 30-second intervals, stirring after each interval, until chocolate is melted and smooth.

2. Beat brown sugar and butter in large bowl until creamy. Add melted chocolate and eggs; beat until well blended. Add flour, applesauce, vanilla, baking soda, baking powder and salt; beat until well blended. Stir in ½ cup chocolate chips. Spoon batter evenly into prepared pans.

3. Bake 35 to 40 minutes or until centers crack and are dry to the touch. Cool in pans on wire racks 10 minutes. Remove from pans; cool completely on wire rack.

4. Place remaining ½ cup chocolate chips and shortening in small microwavable bowl. Microwave on HIGH 1 minute; stir. Microwave at 30-second intervals, stirring after each interval, until chocolate is melted and mixture is smooth. Drizzle loaves with glaze; let stand until set. *Makes 5 mini loaves*

tropical paradise scones

3¼ cups all-purpose flour
½ cup sugar
1 tablespoon plus 1 teaspoon baking powder
¼ teaspoon salt
1 cup MOUNDS® Sweetened Coconut Flakes
1⅓ cups (8-ounce package) HERSHEY'S White Chips and Macadamia Nuts
2 cups chilled whipping cream
2 tablespoons fresh lime juice
2 to 3 teaspoons freshly grated lime peel
2 tablespoons butter, melted
Additional sugar

1. Heat oven to 375°F. Lightly grease 2 baking sheets.

2. Stir together flour, ½ cup sugar, baking powder and salt in large bowl. Stir in coconut and white chips and macadamia nuts.

3. Stir whipping cream, lime juice and lime peel into flour mixture, stirring just until ingredients are moistened.

4. Turn mixture out onto lightly floured surface. Knead gently until soft dough forms (about 2 minutes). Divide dough into three equal balls. One ball at a time, flatten into 7-inch circle; cut into 8 triangles. Transfer triangles to prepared baking sheets, spacing 2 inches apart. Brush with melted butter and sprinkle with additional sugar.

5. Bake 15 to 20 minutes or until lightly browned. Serve warm or cool.   *Makes 24 scones*

apple raisin walnut muffins

2 cups all-purpose flour
¾ cup sugar
2 teaspoons baking powder
1 teaspoon ground cinnamon
½ teaspoon baking soda
½ teaspoon salt
¼ teaspoon ground nutmeg
¾ cup plus 2 tablespoons milk
2 eggs, beaten
⅓ cup butter, melted
1 cup chopped dried apples
½ cup golden raisins
½ cup chopped walnuts

1. Preheat oven to 350°F. Grease 6 jumbo (3½-inch) muffin pan cups. Combine flour, sugar, baking powder, cinnamon, baking soda, salt and nutmeg in large bowl.

2. Beat milk, eggs and butter in small bowl until well blended. Stir into flour mixture just until blended. Gently fold in apples, raisins and walnuts. Spoon batter into prepared muffin cups, filling three-fourths full.

3. Bake 25 to 30 minutes or until toothpick inserted into centers comes out clean. Cool in pan 2 minutes; remove to wire rack. Serve warm or at room temperature.

Makes 6 jumbo muffins

cakes
& cheesecakes

chocolate lovers' cake

Cake

- ¾ cup (1½ sticks) I CAN'T BELIEVE IT'S NOT BUTTER!® Spread
- 6 squares (1 ounce each) bittersweet chocolate, coarsely chopped *or* 1 cup semisweet chocolate chips
- 4 eggs, separated
  Pinch salt
- ¾ cup sugar
- ⅓ cup all-purpose flour

Glaze

- 5 tablespoons I CAN'T BELIEVE IT'S NOT BUTTER!® Spread
- 10 squares (1 ounce each) bittersweet chocolate, coarsely chopped *or* 1⅔ cups semisweet chocolate chips

For cake, preheat oven to 350°F. Grease 9-inch round cake pan, then line with parchment or waxed paper.

In small saucepan, melt I Can't Believe It's Not Butter!® Spread and chocolate over low heat, stirring occasionally; set aside to cool slightly. In medium bowl, with electric mixer, beat egg whites with salt until stiff peaks form.

In medium bowl, with electric mixer, beat egg yolks and sugar until light and ribbony, about 2 minutes. While beating, slowly add chocolate mixture until blended. Beat in flour. With spatula, fold in egg whites just until blended. Pour into prepared pan.

Bake 30 minutes. (Note: Toothpick inserted in center will *not* come out clean.) Remove cake to wire rack and run knife around rim to loosen cake from sides; cool 15 minutes. Remove cake from pan and cool completely.

For glaze, in small saucepan, melt I Can't Believe It's Not Butter! Spread and chocolate in a small saucepan, over low heat, stirring occasionally. Spread warm glaze over cake.

Makes 12 servings

cakes
& cheesecakes

caramel apple cheesecake

1¼ cups graham cracker crumbs
¼ cup (½ stick) butter, melted
3 packages (8 ounces each) cream cheese, softened
¾ cup sugar
1½ teaspoons vanilla
3 eggs
1¼ cups apple pie filling
½ cup chopped peanuts
¼ cup caramel ice cream topping

1. Preheat oven to 350°F. Spray 9-inch springform pan with nonstick cooking spray.

2. Combine graham cracker crumbs and butter in small bowl; press onto bottom of prepared pan. Bake 9 minutes; cool on wire rack.

3. Beat cream cheese, sugar and vanilla in large bowl with electric mixer until well blended. Add eggs, one at a time, beating well after each addition. Pour cream cheese mixture over cooled crust.

4. Bake 40 to 50 minutes or until center is almost set. Cool completely on wire rack. Refrigerate at least 3 hours. Carefully run knife around edge to loosen pan; remove side of pan.

5. Spread apple pie filling over top of cheesecake. Sprinkle peanuts over apple filling; drizzle with caramel topping. Serve immediately. Refrigerate leftovers. *Makes 12 servings*

blueberry crumb cake

    Crumb Topping (recipe follows)
2 cups all-purpose flour
⅔ cup sugar
1 tablespoon baking powder
1 teaspoon salt
½ teaspoon baking soda
1 cup milk
½ cup (1 stick) butter, melted
2 eggs, beaten
2 tablespoons lemon juice
2 cups fresh or thawed frozen blueberries
Crumb Topping (recipe follows)

1. Preheat oven to 375°F. Grease 13×9-inch baking pan. Prepare Crumb Topping; set aside.

2. Sift flour, sugar, baking powder, salt and baking soda into large bowl. Combine milk, butter, eggs and lemon juice in medium bowl. Add milk mixture to flour mixture; stir until well blended.

3. Pour batter into prepared pan; top with blueberries. Sprinkle evenly with Crumb Topping. Bake 40 to 45 minutes or until toothpick inserted into center comes out clean. Serve warm.   *Makes 12 to 16 servings*

Crumb Topping: Combine 1 cup chopped walnuts or pecans, ⅔ cup sugar, ½ cup all-purpose flour, ¼ cup (½ stick) softened butter and ½ teaspoon ground cinnamon in large bowl until mixture forms coarse crumbs.

lemon-up cakes

1 package (18¼ ounces) butter recipe white cake mix with pudding in the mix, plus ingredients to prepare mix
½ cup fresh lemon juice, divided (2 large lemons)
Grated peel of 2 lemons, divided
½ cup (1 stick) butter, softened
3½ cups powdered sugar
Yellow food coloring
1 package (9½ ounces) lemon-shaped hard candies, coarsely crushed

1. Preheat oven to 350°F. Line 24 standard (2½-inch) muffin pan cups with paper baking cups.

2. Prepare cake mix according to package directions but use ¼ cup less water than directions call for. Stir in ¼ cup lemon juice and half of grated lemon peel. Spoon batter evenly into prepared muffin cups.

3. Bake 23 minutes or until light golden brown and toothpick inserted into centers comes out clean. Cool cupcakes in pans on wire racks 5 minutes; remove from pans and cool completely on wire racks.

4. Beat butter in large bowl with electric mixer at medium speed until creamy. Gradually add powdered sugar. Add remaining ¼ cup lemon juice, lemon peel and several drops food coloring; beat at high speed until frosting is light and fluffy.

5. Generously frost cupcakes. Sprinkle crushed candies over frosting. *Makes 24 cupcakes*

tip | One medium lemon will yield about 3 to 4 tablespoons of juice and 1 to 2 teaspoons of grated peel. To get the most juice from your lemons, warm them to room temperature and press down as you roll them on the countertop with the palm of your hand before squeezing.

orange kiss me cakes

1 large orange
1 cup raisins
⅔ cup chopped walnuts, divided
2 cups all-purpose flour
1⅓ cups sugar, divided
1 teaspoon baking soda
1 teaspoon salt
1 cup milk, divided
½ cup shortening
2 eggs
1 teaspoon ground cinnamon

1. Preheat oven to 350°F. Lightly grease and flour 6 (1-cup) mini bundt pans or 1 (12-cup) bundt pan.

2. Juice orange; reserve ⅓ cup juice. Coarsely chop remaining orange pulp and peel. Process pulp, peel, raisins and ⅓ cup walnuts in food processor fitted with metal blade until finely ground.

3. Sift flour, 1 cup sugar, baking soda and salt into large bowl. Add ¾ cup milk and shortening; beat with electric mixer at medium speed 2 minutes or until well blended. Beat 2 minutes more. Add eggs and remaining ¼ cup milk; beat 2 minutes. Fold orange mixture into batter; mix well. Pour into prepared pans.

4. Bake 40 to 45 minutes or until toothpick inserted near centers comes out clean. Cool in pan 15 minutes. Invert onto serving plate. Poke holes in cakes with wooden skewer or tines of fork.

5. Pour reserved orange juice over warm cakes. Combine remaining ⅓ cup sugar, ⅓ cup walnuts and cinnamon in small bowl. Sprinkle over cakes. Garnish as desired.   *Makes 6 cakes*

toffee crunch cheesecake

Crust

> **8 ounces chocolate cookies or vanilla wafers, crushed**
> **¼ cup (½ stick) butter, melted**

Filling

> **3 packages (8 ounces each) cream cheese, softened**
> **½ cup granulated sugar**
> **¼ cup packed light brown sugar**
> **3 eggs**
> **1¾ cups (10-ounce package) toffee baking bits, divided**
> **1¼ teaspoons vanilla**
> **Sweetened whipped cream**

1. Preheat oven to 350°F. For crust, combine cookie crumbs and butter; press onto bottom of 9-inch springform pan.

2. For filling, beat cream cheese, granulated sugar and brown sugar in large bowl with electric mixer until smooth. Add eggs, one at a time, beating well after each addition. Reserve 1 tablespoon toffee bits. Gently stir remaining toffee bits and vanilla into batter; pour into prepared crust.

3. Bake 45 to 50 minutes or until almost set. Remove to wire rack. Carefully run knife around edge of pan to loosen cheesecake from pan. Cool completely before removing side of pan. Cover and refrigerate. Just before serving, garnish with whipped cream and reserved toffee bits. *Makes 10 to 12 servings*

jo's moist and delicious chocolate cake

       2 cups all-purpose flour
       1 cup sugar
     ¼ cup unsweetened cocoa powder
    1½ teaspoons baking powder
    1½ teaspoons baking soda
       1 cup mayonnaise
       1 cup hot coffee
       2 teaspoons vanilla

1. Preheat oven to 350°F. Grease and flour 12-cup (10-inch) bundt pan.

2. Sift flour, sugar, cocoa, baking powder and baking soda into large bowl. Stir in mayonnaise, coffee and vanilla until smooth and well blended. Pour batter into prepared pan.

3. Bake 30 minutes or until toothpick inserted near center comes out clean. Cool on wire rack 10 to 15 minutes. Remove cake from pan; cool completely on wire rack.   *Makes 12 servings*

Tip: Frost cake with your favorite icing or glaze, or sprinkle with powdered sugar.

easy apple cake

       4 apples, peeled, cored and thinly sliced
    1½ cups granulated sugar, divided
     ½ teaspoon ground cinnamon
       2 cups all-purpose flour
     ¾ cup vegetable oil
       3 eggs, beaten
       1 tablespoon plus 2 teaspoons lemon juice
    1½ teaspoons baking soda
       1 teaspoon vanilla
         Powdered sugar

1. Preheat oven to 325°F. Grease 13×9-inch baking pan.

2. Combine apples, ½ cup granulated sugar and cinnamon in medium bowl. Combine flour, remaining 1 cup granulated sugar, oil, eggs, lemon juice, baking soda and vanilla in large bowl. Add apple mixture; stir until well blended. Pour into prepared pan.

3. Bake 35 to 40 minutes or until toothpick inserted into center comes out clean. Cool in pan on wire rack; sprinkle with powered sugar.   *Makes 12 servings*

cocoa cheesecake

    Graham Crust (recipe follows)
  2 packages (8 ounces each) cream cheese, softened
 ¾ cup plus 2 tablespoons sugar, divided
 ½ cup HERSHEY'S Cocoa
  2 teaspoons vanilla extract, divided
  2 eggs
  1 container (8 ounces) dairy sour cream
    Fresh fruit, sliced

1. Prepare Graham Crust. Heat oven to 375°F.

2. Beat cream cheese, ¾ cup sugar, cocoa and 1 teaspoon vanilla in large bowl until well blended. Add eggs; blend well. Pour batter into Graham Crust. Bake 20 minutes. Remove from oven; cool 15 minutes. Increase oven temperature to 425°F.

3. Stir together sour cream, remaining 2 tablespoons sugar and remaining 1 teaspoon vanilla in small bowl until smooth; spread evenly over top of cheesecake.

4. Bake 10 minutes; remove from oven. Loosen cheesecake from side of pan; cool to room temperature. Refrigerate several hours or overnight; remove side of pan. Garnish with fresh fruit. Cover; refrigerate leftover cheesecake.   *Makes 10 to 12 servings*

Graham Crust: Combine 1½ cups graham cracker crumbs, ⅓ cup sugar and ⅓ cup melted butter or margarine in small bowl. Press mixture onto bottom and halfway up side of 9-inch springform pan.

Chocolate Lover's Cheesecake: Prepare batter as directed above; stir 1 cup HERSHEY'S Semi-Sweet Chocolate Chips into batter before pouring into crust. Bake and serve as directed.

chocolate-peanut butter oatmeal snacking cake

1 cup uncooked old-fashioned oats
1¼ cups boiling water
1 cup granulated sugar
1 cup packed brown sugar
½ cup (1 stick) butter, softened
2 eggs, beaten
1 teaspoon vanilla
1¾ cups all-purpose flour
¼ cup unsweetened cocoa powder
1 teaspoon baking soda
1 cup semisweet chocolate chips
1 package (12 ounces) chocolate and peanut butter chips

1. Preheat oven to 350°F. Grease 13×9-inch baking pan.

2. Combine oats and boiling water in large bowl; let stand 10 minutes. Stir until water is absorbed. Add granulated sugar, brown sugar and butter; beat with electric mixer at low speed 1 minute or until well blended. Beat in eggs and vanilla.

3. Combine flour, cocoa and baking soda in medium bowl. Gradually beat into oat mixture until well blended. Stir in 1 cup chocolate chips. Pour into prepared pan. Sprinkle with chocolate and peanut butter chips.

4. Bake 40 minutes. Cool completely in pan on wire rack. *Makes 16 to 20 servings*

raspberry swirl cheesecakes

1½ cups fresh or frozen red raspberries, thawed
1 (14-ounce) can EAGLE BRAND® Sweetened Condensed Milk (NOT evaporated milk), divided
2 (8-ounce) packages cream cheese, softened
3 eggs
2 (6-ounce) prepared chocolate crumb pie crusts
   Chocolate and white chocolate leaves (recipe follows, optional)
   Fresh raspberries for garnish (optional)

1. Preheat oven to 350°F. In blender container, blend 1½ cups raspberries until smooth; press through sieve to remove seeds. Stir ⅓ cup EAGLE BRAND® into raspberry purée; set aside.

2. In large bowl, beat cream cheese, eggs and remaining EAGLE BRAND® until smooth. Spoon into crusts. Drizzle with raspberry mixture. With table knife, gently swirl raspberry mixture through cream cheese mixture.

3. Bake 25 minutes or until centers are nearly set when shaken. Cool. Cover and chill at least 4 hours. Garnish with chocolate leaves and fresh raspberries (optional). Store leftovers covered in refrigerator.

Makes two cheesecakes

Chocolate Leaves: Place 1 (1-ounce) square semisweet or white chocolate in microwave-safe bowl. Microwave at HIGH (100% power) 1 to 2 minutes, stirring every minute until smooth. With small, clean paintbrush, paint several coats of melted chocolate on undersides of nontoxic leaves, such as mint, lemon or strawberry. Wipe off any chocolate from top sides of leaves. Place leaves, chocolate sides up, on wax-paper-lined baking sheet or on curved surface, such as rolling pin. Refrigerate leaves until chocolate is firm. To use, carefully peel leaves away from chocolate.

Prep Time: 15 minutes
Bake Time: 25 minutes
Chill Time: 4 hours

raspberry swirl cheesecake

warm chocolate cakes

4 ounces bittersweet or semisweet chocolate
½ cup (1 stick) butter
2 eggs
2 egg yolks
¼ cup granulated sugar
¼ cup all-purpose flour
¼ teaspoon salt
Powdered sugar (optional)

1. Preheat oven to 400°F. Butter 4 (¾-cup) custard cups or soufflé dishes; place on baking sheet.

2. Melt chocolate and butter in small saucepan over very low heat; cool slightly. Meanwhile, beat eggs, egg yolks and granulated sugar in large bowl with electric mixer about 5 minutes or until thick and light in color.

3. Add flour and salt; beat just until blended. Gently fold in chocolate mixture. Pour into prepared custard cups.

4. Bake about 9 minutes or until edges of cakes are set but centers are soft and move slightly when shaken. Let stand 2 minutes; invert cakes onto individual plates. Sprinkle with powdered sugar.   *Makes 4 cakes*

Tip: The cakes can be made several hours in advance and baked just before serving. Prepare batter as directed; cover and refrigerate until ready to bake. Bake at 400°F 10 to 11 minutes.

peach streusel coffeecake

2½ cups biscuit baking mix, divided
⅔ cup whole milk
1 egg
¼ cup granulated sugar
1 teaspoon ground cinnamon
1 teaspoon vanilla
1 pound frozen unsweetened peaches, thawed and diced
½ cup packed dark brown sugar
½ cup pecan pieces
3 tablespoons cold butter, diced

1. Preheat oven to 375°F. Spray 9-inch square baking pan with nonstick cooking spray.

2. For coffeecake, place 2 cups baking mix in medium bowl; break up lumps with spoon. Add milk, egg, granulated sugar, cinnamon and vanilla; stir until well blended. Add peaches; stir just until blended. Pour batter into prepared pan.

3. For topping, combine remaining ½ cup baking mix and brown sugar in small bowl; stir until well blended. Add pecans and butter; toss gently (do not break up small pieces of butter). Sprinkle evenly over batter.

4. Bake 35 minutes or until toothpick inserted into center comes out clean. Let stand 15 minutes or cool completely before serving.

Makes 9 servings

banana cake

2½ cups all-purpose flour
1 tablespoon baking soda
½ teaspoon salt
1 cup granulated sugar
¾ cup packed light brown sugar
½ cup (1 stick) butter, softened
2 eggs
1 teaspoon vanilla
3 ripe bananas, mashed (about 1⅔ cups)
⅔ cup buttermilk
1 container (16 ounces) dark chocolate frosting

1. Preheat oven to 350°F. Grease 2 (8-inch) round cake pans.

2. Combine flour, baking soda and salt in large bowl. Beat granulated sugar, brown sugar and butter in medium bowl with electric mixer until well blended. Add eggs and vanilla; beat well. Stir in bananas. Add flour mixture and buttermilk alternately to banana mixture. Pour batter into prepared pans.

3. Bake about 35 minutes or until toothpick inserted into centers comes out clean. Cool in pans 10 minutes. Remove from pans; cool completely on wire racks.

4. Fill and frost cake with chocolate frosting.

Makes 12 to 16 servings

chocolate chip cheesecake

Crust

1½ cups (about 15) crushed chocolate sandwich cookies

2 tablespoons butter or margarine, melted

2 cups (12-ounce package) NESTLÉ® TOLL HOUSE® Semi-Sweet Chocolate Mini Morsels, *divided*

Filling

2 packages (8 ounces *each*) cream cheese, softened

½ cup granulated sugar

1 tablespoon vanilla extract

2 large eggs

2 tablespoons all-purpose flour

¾ cup NESTLÉ® CARNATION® Evaporated Milk

½ cup sour cream

For Crust

PREHEAT oven to 300°F.

COMBINE cookie crumbs and butter in medium bowl until moistened; press onto bottom of ungreased 9-inch springform pan. Sprinkle with *1 cup* morsels.

For Filling

BEAT cream cheese, sugar and vanilla extract in large mixer bowl until smooth. Beat in eggs and flour. Gradually beat in evaporated milk and sour cream. Pour over crust. Sprinkle with *remaining* morsels.

BAKE for 25 minutes. Cover loosely with aluminum foil. Bake for additional 30 to 40 minutes or until edge is set but center still moves slightly. Place in refrigerator immediately; refrigerate for 2 hours or until firm. Remove side of springform pan. *Makes 12 to 14 servings*

Note: Cheesecake may be baked in 13×9-inch pan. Prepare as above. Bake in preheated 300°F oven for 20 minutes. Cover loosely with aluminum foil. Bake for additional 20 to 30 minutes.

spicy applesauce cake

2¼ cups all-purpose flour
2 teaspoons baking soda
1 teaspoon ground cinnamon
1 teaspoon ground nutmeg
½ teaspoon ground cloves
1 cup firmly packed brown sugar
½ cup FILIPPO BERIO® Olive Oil
1½ cups applesauce
1 cup raisins
1 cup coarsely chopped walnuts
Powdered sugar or sweetened whipped cream (optional)

Preheat oven to 375°F. Grease 9-inch square pan with olive oil. In medium bowl, combine flour, baking soda, cinnamon, nutmeg and cloves.

In large bowl, mix brown sugar and olive oil with electric mixer at medium speed until blended. Add applesauce; mix well. Add flour mixture all at once; beat at low speed until well blended. Stir in raisins and nuts. Spoon batter into prepared pan.

Bake 20 to 25 minutes or until lightly browned. Cool completely on wire rack. Cut into squares. Serve plain, dusted with powdered sugar or frosted with whipped cream, if desired. *Makes 9 servings*

cranberry pound cake

1 cup (2 sticks) unsalted butter
1½ cups sugar
¼ teaspoon salt
¼ teaspoon mace
4 eggs
2 cups cake flour
1 cup chopped fresh or frozen cranberries

1. Preheat oven to 350°F. Grease and flour 9×5-inch loaf pan.

2. Beat butter, sugar, salt and mace in large bowl with electric mixer at medium speed until light and fluffy. Beat in eggs, one at a time, until well blended. Reduce speed to low; add flour, ½ cup at a time, scraping down bowl occasionally. Fold in cranberries.

3. Spoon batter into prepared pan. Bake 60 to 70 minutes or until toothpick inserted near center comes out clean. Cool in pan on wire rack 5 minutes. Run knife around edges of pan to loosen cake; cool additional 30 minutes in pan. Remove from pan; cool completely on wire rack.   *Makes 12 servings*

tip | If fresh or frozen cranberries aren't available, you can still make this delicious pound cake. Cover 1 cup dried sweetened cranberries with hot water and let stand 10 minutes. Drain well before folding them into the batter.

cranberry pound cake

individual chocolate coconut cheesecakes

1 cup chocolate cookie crumbs
¼ cup (½ stick) butter, melted
2 packages (8 ounces each) cream cheese, softened
⅓ cup sugar
2 eggs
1 teaspoon vanilla
¼ teaspoon coconut extract (optional)
½ cup flaked coconut
½ cup semisweet chocolate chips
1 teaspoon shortening

1. Preheat oven to 325°F. Line 12 standard (2½-inch) muffin pan cups with foil or paper baking cups.

2. Combine cookie crumbs and butter in small bowl. Press onto bottoms of baking cups.

3. Beat cream cheese and sugar in large bowl with electric mixer at medium speed 2 minutes or until well blended. Add eggs, vanilla and coconut extract, if desired; beat just until blended. Stir in coconut.

4. Carefully spoon about ¼ cup cream cheese mixture into each baking cup. Bake 18 to 22 minutes or until nearly set. Cool 30 minutes in pan on wire rack. Remove from pan. Peel away foil baking cups.

5. Melt chocolate chips and shortening in small saucepan over low heat, stirring frequently, until chocolate is melted. Drizzle over cheesecakes. Let stand 20 minutes. Refrigerate until ready to serve.

Makes 12 servings

carrot snack cake

1 package (18¼ ounces) butter recipe yellow cake mix with pudding in the mix, plus ingredients to prepare mix

2 jars (4 ounces each) strained carrot baby food

1½ cups chopped walnuts, divided

1 cup shredded carrots

½ cup golden raisins

1½ teaspoons ground cinnamon

1½ teaspoons vanilla, divided

1 package (8 ounces) cream cheese, softened

Grated peel of 1 lemon

2 teaspoons fresh lemon juice

3 cups powdered sugar

1. Preheat oven to 350°F. Grease 13×9-inch baking pan.

2. Prepare cake mix according to package directions but use only ½ cup water instead of amount directions call for. Stir carrot baby food, 1 cup walnuts, carrots, raisins, cinnamon and ½ teaspoon vanilla into batter. Spread in prepared pan.

3. Bake 40 minutes or until cake begins to pull away from sides of pan and toothpick inserted into center comes out clean. Cool completely in pan on wire rack.

4. Beat cream cheese in large bowl with electric mixer until fluffy. Beat in lemon peel, lemon juice and remaining 1 teaspoon vanilla. Gradually add powdered sugar, scraping down side of bowl occasionally; beat until well blended and smooth. Spread frosting over cooled cake; sprinkle with remaining ½ cup walnuts. Refrigerate 2 hours before serving. *Makes 24 servings*

toffee-topped pineapple upside-down cakes

¼ cup light corn syrup
¼ cup (½ stick) butter or margarine, melted
1 cup HEATH® BITS 'O BRICKLE® Toffee Bits
4 pineapple rings
4 maraschino cherries
¼ cup (½ stick) butter or margarine, softened
⅔ cup sugar
1 egg
1 tablespoon rum or 1 teaspoon rum extract
1⅓ cups all-purpose flour
2 teaspoons baking powder
⅔ cup milk

1. Heat oven to 350°F. Lightly coat inside of 4 individual 2-cup baking dishes with vegetable oil spray.

2. Stir together 1 tablespoon corn syrup and 1 tablespoon melted butter in each of 4 baking dishes. Sprinkle each with ¼ cup toffee. Center pineapple rings over toffee and place cherries in centers.

3. Beat softened butter and sugar in small bowl until blended. Add egg and rum, beating well. Stir together flour and baking powder; add alternately with milk to sugar mixture, beating until smooth. Spoon about ¾ cup batter into each prepared dish.

4. Bake 25 to 30 minutes or until wooden pick inserted in centers comes out clean. Immediately invert onto serving dishes. Refrigerate leftovers.

Makes four 4-inch cakes

delectable desserts

cranberry apple crisp

½ cup KARO® Light Corn Syrup
⅓ to ½ cup granulated sugar
1 teaspoon cinnamon
½ teaspoon nutmeg
5 to 6 cups cubed, peeled tart apples
1 cup fresh or frozen cranberries
3 tablespoons ARGO® or KINGSFORD'S® Corn Starch
1 teaspoon grated orange peel

Topping

½ cup walnuts or uncooked oats
⅓ cup packed brown sugar
¼ cup flour
¼ cup (½ stick) margarine or butter

Preheat oven to 350°F.

In large bowl combine corn syrup, granulated sugar, cinnamon and nutmeg. Add apples, cranberries, corn starch and orange peel; toss to mix well. Spoon into shallow 2-quart baking dish.

For topping, combine nuts, brown sugar and flour. With pastry blender or 2 knives, cut in margarine until crumbly. Sprinkle over cranberry mixture.

Bake 50 minutes or until apples are tender and juices that bubble up in center are shiny and clear. Cool slightly; serve warm.

Makes 8 servings

Prep Time: 25 minutes
Bake Time: 50 minutes

delectable
desserts

pumpkin crème brulée

1 cup whipping cream
1 cup half-and-half
½ cup granulated sugar
¼ teaspoon salt
¼ teaspoon ground cinnamon
   Pinch ground nutmeg (optional)
4 egg yolks
½ cup solid-pack pumpkin
¼ cup packed light brown sugar

1. Preheat oven to 300°F. Coat 4 (1-cup) ramekins or custard cups with nonstick cooking spray. Combine cream, half-and-half, granulated sugar, salt, cinnamon and nutmeg in medium saucepan. Bring to a simmer over medium-high heat.

2. Beat egg yolks in heatproof bowl. Gradually whisk in one fourth of hot cream mixture. Slowly pour egg mixture back into remaining hot cream mixture in saucepan, whisking constantly until slightly thickened. Remove from heat; stir in pumpkin until well blended.

3. Pour pumpkin mixture into prepared ramekins. Place ramekins in 9-inch square baking pan; carefully add hot water to pan to depth of 1 inch. Bake 45 to 55 minutes or until crème brulées are set. Cool in pan 30 minutes. Remove from pan and chill at least 1 hour.

4. Preheat broiler. Sprinkle 1 tablespoon brown sugar over each crème brulée to thinly cover surface. Place ramekins on baking sheet. Broil 4 inches from heat 1 minute or until sugar melts. Cool 15 minutes before serving.

Makes 4 servings

s'more bundles

1¼ cups mini marshmallows
1¼ cups semisweet chocolate chips
1¼ cups coarsely crushed graham crackers (5 whole graham crackers)
1 package (17¼ ounces) frozen puff pastry, thawed

1. Preheat oven to 400°F. Combine marshmallows, chocolate chips and graham crackers in medium bowl.

2. Unfold pastry on lightly floured surface. Roll each pastry sheet into 12-inch square; cut into 4 (6-inch) squares. Place scant ½ cup marshmallow mixture in center of each square.

3. Brush edges of pastry squares with water. Bring edges together over filling; twist tightly to seal. Place bundles 2 inches apart on ungreased baking sheets.

4. Bake about 20 minutes or until golden brown. Cool 5 minutes on wire rack.

Makes 8 servings

blueberry crisp

1 can (21 ounces) blueberry pie filling
⅔ cup all-purpose flour
⅔ cup firmly packed light brown sugar
½ cup quick cooking oats
½ teaspoon ground cinnamon
½ cup HELLMANN'S® or BEST FOODS® Real Mayonnaise

1. Preheat oven to 375°F. In shallow 8×8-inch baking dish, spoon pie filling.

2. In medium bowl, combine flour, brown sugar, oats and cinnamon. Stir in Hellmann's or Best Foods Real Mayonnaise. Using fingers, gently squeeze dough to form crumbs. Evenly sprinkle crumbs over pie filling.

3. Bake 30 minutes or until topping is golden.

Makes 8 servings

Prep Time: 8 minutes
Bake Time: 30 minutes

plum bread pudding

6 cups 1-inch egg bread* cubes
6 large Italian plums, unpeeled
1 tablespoon butter
¾ cup plus 1 tablespoon sugar, divided
6 eggs
2 cups half-and-half
1 cup milk
1 teaspoon vanilla
½ teaspoon salt
½ teaspoon ground cinnamon
Heavy cream or vanilla ice cream (optional)

*Use an egg-rich bread, such as challah, for best results. For a more delicate bread pudding, substitute cinnamon rolls or plain Danish rolls.

1. Preheat oven to 400°F. Lightly coat 9-inch square glass baking dish with nonstick cooking spray.

2. Spread bread cubes on ungreased baking sheet. Bake 6 to 7 minutes until lightly toasted, turning bread over halfway through baking time. Set aside to cool. *Reduce oven temperature to 325°F.*

3. Pit plums and cut into thin wedges. Melt butter in large skillet. Add plums and 1 tablespoon sugar; cook over high heat 2 minutes or until plums are soft. Remove from heat.

4. Beat eggs, half-and-half, milk, remaining ¾ cup sugar, vanilla, salt and cinnamon in large bowl. Stir in bread cubes, plums and any juices. Spoon into prepared baking dish.

5. Bake 60 to 65 minutes or until pudding is firm when gently shaken and knife inserted halfway between center and edge comes out clean. Remove from oven. Cool 15 minutes. Serve with cream or ice cream, if desired.

Makes 6 to 8 servings

banana split ice cream sandwiches

1 package (18 ounces) refrigerated chocolate chip cookie dough
2 ripe bananas, mashed
½ cup strawberry jam, divided
4 cups strawberry ice cream (or any flavor), softened
   Hot fudge topping and whipped cream (optional)
9 maraschino cherries (optional)

1. Preheat oven to 350°F. Lightly grease 13×9-inch baking pan. Let dough stand at room temperature about 15 minutes.

2. Beat dough and bananas in large bowl until well blended. Spread dough evenly in prepared pan and smooth top. Bake about 22 minutes or until edges are light brown. Cool completely in pan on wire rack.

3. Line 8-inch square baking pan with foil or plastic wrap, allowing some to hang over edges of pan. Remove cooled cookie from pan; cut in half crosswise. Place 1 cookie half, top side down, in prepared pan, trimming edges to fit, if necessary. Spread ¼ cup jam evenly over cookie in pan. Spread ice cream evenly over jam. Spread remaining ¼ cup jam over bottom of remaining cookie half; place jam side down over ice cream. Wrap tightly with foil; freeze at least 2 hours or overnight.

4. Cut into bars and top with hot fudge sauce, whipped cream and cherries, if desired.   *Makes 9 servings*

 tip | Overripe bananas aren't good for eating, but they add great flavor to baked goods. Brown speckles on the skin are an indication of ripeness, and when the skins develop black patches, the bananas are overripe. Bananas with green tips and ridges will ripen at room temperature within a day or two. To speed ripening, place the bananas in an unsealed paper bag at room temperature.

black forest tarts

1 package (18 ounces) refrigerated triple chocolate cookie dough
⅓ cup unsweetened cocoa powder
1 can (21 ounces) cherry pie filling
3 squares (1 ounce each) white chocolate, finely chopped

1. Preheat oven to 350°F. Lightly grease 18 standard (2½-inch) muffin pan cups or line with foil baking cups. Let dough stand at room temperature about 15 minutes.

2. Beat dough and cocoa in large bowl until well blended. Shape dough into 18 balls; press onto bottoms and up sides of prepared muffin cups.

3. Bake about 15 minutes or until set. Remove from oven; gently press down center of each cookie cup with back of teaspoon. Cool in pans 10 minutes. Remove cookie cups from pans; cool completely on wire racks.

4. Place 1 tablespoon cherry pie filling in each cookie cup.

5. Place white chocolate in small resealable food storage bag. Microwave on MEDIUM (50%) 1 minute; knead bag lightly. Microwave and knead at additional 30-second intervals until white chocolate is completely melted. Cut off tiny corner of bag; drizzle white chocolate over tarts. Let stand until set. *Makes 1½ dozen tarts*

berry-peachy cobbler

4 tablespoons plus 2 teaspoons sugar, divided

¾ cup plus 2 tablespoons all-purpose flour

1¼ pounds peaches, peeled and sliced *or* **1 package (16 ounces) frozen unsweetened sliced peaches, thawed and drained**

2 cups fresh raspberries *or* **1 package (12 ounces) frozen unsweetened raspberries**

1 teaspoon grated lemon peel

½ teaspoon baking powder

½ teaspoon baking soda

⅛ teaspoon salt

2 tablespoons cold butter, cut into small pieces

½ cup buttermilk

1. Preheat oven to 425°F. Spray 8 ramekins or 11×7-inch baking dish with nonstick cooking spray; place ramekins on jelly-roll pan.

2. For filling, combine 2 tablespoons sugar and 2 tablespoons flour in large bowl. Add peaches, raspberries and lemon peel; toss to coat. Divide fruit among prepared ramekins. Bake about 15 minutes or until fruit is bubbly around edges.

3. Meanwhile, for topping, combine remaining ¾ cup flour, 2 tablespoons sugar, baking powder, baking soda and salt in medium bowl. Cut in butter using pastry blender or two knives until mixture resembles coarse crumbs. Stir in buttermilk just until dry ingredients are moistened.

4. Remove ramekins from oven; top fruit with equal dollops of topping. Sprinkle topping with remaining 2 teaspoons sugar. Bake 18 to 20 minutes or until topping is lightly browned. Serve warm.

Makes 8 servings

rustic cranberry-pear galette

¼ **cup sugar, divided**
1 **tablespoon plus 1 teaspoon cornstarch**
2 **teaspoons ground cinnamon or apple pie spice**
4 **cups thinly sliced, peeled Bartlett pears**
¼ **cup dried cranberries**
1 **teaspoon vanilla**
¼ **teaspoon almond extract (optional)**
1 **refrigerated pie crust, at room temperature (half of 15-ounce package)**
1 **egg white**
1 **tablespoon water**

1. Preheat oven to 450°F. Spray pizza pan or baking sheet with nonstick cooking spray.

2. Reserve 1 teaspoon sugar. Combine remaining sugar, cornstarch and cinnamon in medium bowl; mix well. Add pears, cranberries, vanilla and almond extract; toss to coat.

3. Place crust on prepared pan. Spoon pear mixture into center of crust to within 2 inches of edge. Fold edge of crust 2 inches over pear mixture; crimp slightly.

4. Combine egg white and water in small bowl; whisk until well blended. Brush outer edge of pie crust with egg white mixture; sprinkle with reserved 1 teaspoon sugar.

5. Bake 25 minutes or until pears are tender and crust is golden brown. If crust browns too quickly, cover with foil after 15 minutes of baking. Cool on wire rack 30 minutes. *Makes 8 servings*

toffee bread pudding with cinnamon toffee sauce

1⅓ cups (8-ounce package) HEATH® BITS 'O BRICKLE® Toffee Bits, divided
  3 cups milk
  4 eggs
¾ cup sugar
¾ teaspoon ground cinnamon
¾ teaspoon vanilla extract
½ teaspoon salt
6 to 6½ cups ½-inch cubes French, Italian or sourdough bread
    Cinnamon Toffee Sauce (recipe follows)
    Sweetened whipped cream or ice cream (optional)

1. Heat oven to 350°F. Butter 13×9×2-inch baking pan. Set aside ¾ cup toffee bits for sauce.

2. Mix together milk, eggs, sugar, cinnamon, vanilla and salt in large bowl with wire whisk. Stir in bread cubes, coating completely. Allow to stand 10 minutes. Stir in remaining toffee bits. Pour into prepared pan.

3. Bake 40 to 45 minutes or until surface is set. Cool 30 minutes.

4. Meanwhile, prepare Cinnamon Toffee Sauce. Cut pudding into squares; top with sauce and sweetened whipped cream or ice cream, if desired.
Makes 12 servings

Cinnamon Toffee Sauce: Combine ¾ cup reserved toffee bits, ⅓ cup whipping cream and ⅛ teaspoon ground cinnamon in medium saucepan. Cook over low heat, stirring constantly, until toffee melts and mixture is well blended. (As toffee melts, small bits of almond will remain.) Makes about ⅔ cup sauce.

Note: This dessert is best eaten the same day it is prepared.

toffee bread pudding with
cinnamon toffee sauce

easy peach buckle

   1 package (16 ounces) frozen peach slices *or* 2½ cups fresh peach slices
¾ cup water
   2 tablespoons sugar
¾ cup plus 2 tablespoons all-pupose flour
¼ cup packed brown sugar
   1 teaspoon baking powder
¾ teaspoon ground cinnamon
½ teaspoon baking soda
⅛ teaspoon salt
⅔ cup buttermilk
   3 tablespoons canola or vegetable oil
½ teaspoon vanilla

1. Preheat oven to 375°F. Lightly grease 1½-quart baking dish.

2. Combine peaches and water in medium saucepan. Bring to a boil over high heat; reduce heat and simmer 3 minutes. Remove from heat; stir in sugar.

3. Combine flour, brown sugar, baking powder, cinnamon, baking soda and salt in medium bowl. Combine buttermilk, oil and vanilla in small bowl; mix well. Stir into flour mixture just until blended.

4. Spread batter evenly into prepared baking dish. Arrange peaches over batter; carefully pour liquid evenly over peaches. Bake about 30 minutes or until lightly browned and cake springs back when touched. Serve warm.   *Makes 6 servings*

plum-ginger bruschetta

1 sheet frozen puff pastry (half of 17¼-ounce package)
2 cups chopped, unpeeled firm ripe plums (about 3 medium)
2 tablespoons sugar
2 tablespoons chopped candied ginger
1 tablespoon all-purpose flour
2 teaspoons lemon juice
⅛ teaspoon ground cinnamon
2 tablespoons apple or apricot jelly

1. Unfold puff pastry and thaw 30 minutes on lightly floured work surface. Preheat oven to 400°F. Line baking sheet with parchment paper.

2. Cut puff pastry sheet lengthwise into 3 strips. Cut each strip crosswise in thirds for total of 9 pieces. Place on prepared baking sheet; puff pastry pieces should just touch. Bake 10 minutes or until puffed and lightly browned.

3. Meanwhile, combine plums, sugar, ginger, flour, lemon juice and cinnamon in medium bowl.

4. Remove puff pastry from oven. Gently brush each piece with about ½ teaspoon jelly; top with scant ¼ cup plum mixture. Bake about 12 minutes or until fruit is tender. *Makes 9 servings*

best-ever baked rice pudding

   3 eggs
⅓ cup sugar
¼ teaspoon salt
   2 cups milk
   2 cups *cooked* rice
½ cup golden raisins
      Grated peel of 1 SUNKIST® lemon
      Warm Lemon Sauce (recipe follows)

In large bowl, beat eggs slightly with sugar and salt. Stir in milk, rice, raisins and lemon peel. Pour into well-buttered 1-quart casserole. Bake, uncovered, at 325°F 50 to 60 minutes or until set. Serve with Warm Lemon Sauce. Refrigerate leftovers.   *Makes 6 servings (about 3½ cups)*

warm lemon sauce

⅓ cup sugar
   2 tablespoons cornstarch
⅛ teaspoon salt
      Dash nutmeg (optional)
¾ cup water
      Grated peel of ½ SUNKIST® lemon
      Juice of 1 SUNKIST® lemon
   1 tablespoon butter or margarine
      Few drops yellow food coloring (optional)

In small saucepan, combine sugar, cornstarch, salt and nutmeg. Gradually blend in water, lemon peel and juice. Add butter. Cook over medium heat, stirring until thickened. Stir in food coloring. Serve warm.
Makes about 1 cup

double cherry crumbles

½ **(18-ounce) package refrigerated oatmeal raisin cookie dough***
½ **cup uncooked old-fashioned oats**
¾ **teaspoon ground cinnamon**
½ **teaspoon ground ginger**
2 **tablespoons cold butter, cut into small pieces**
1 **cup chopped pecans, toasted****
1 **bag (16 ounces) frozen pitted unsweetened dark sweet cherries, thawed**
2 **cans (21 ounces each) cherry pie filling**

*Save remaining half package of dough for another use.

**To toast pecans, spread in single layer on baking sheet. Bake in preheated 350°F oven 7 to 10 minutes or until golden brown, stirring frequently.

1. Preheat oven to 350°F. Lightly grease 8 (½-cup) ramekins; place on baking sheet. Let dough stand at room temperature about 15 minutes.

2. For topping, beat dough, oats, cinnamon and ginger in large bowl until well blended. Cut in butter with pastry blender or 2 knives. Stir in pecans.

3. Combine cherries and pie filling in large bowl; mix well. Divide cherry mixture evenly among prepared ramekins; sprinkle with topping. Bake about 25 minutes or until topping is browned. Serve warm.

Makes 8 servings

plum cobbler with cinnamon drop biscuits

6 cups sliced, unpeeled plums (about 12 medium)
1 cup plus 2 tablespoons all-purpose flour, divided
8 tablespoons granulated sugar, divided
¼ cup packed brown sugar
1 tablespoon lemon juice
2 teaspoons baking powder
½ teaspoon ground cinnamon
¼ teaspoon salt
¼ cup (½ stick) cold butter, cubed
8 to 10 tablespoons milk

1. Preheat oven to 400°F. Butter 8-inch square baking dish.

2. Combine plum slices, 2 tablespoons flour, 6 tablespoons granulated sugar, brown sugar and lemon juice in large bowl. Toss to coat fruit evenly. Spoon fruit into baking dish. Bake 10 minutes.

3. Meanwhile, combine remaining 1 cup flour, 2 tablespoons granulated sugar, baking powder, cinnamon and salt in medium bowl. Cut in butter with pastry blender or two knives until mixture resembles coarse crumbs. Add milk, one tablespoon at a time, stirring gently until sticky dough forms. Remove fruit from oven. Drop heaping tablespoons of batter onto fruit. Bake 20 minutes or until fruit is bubbling and biscuits are crusty and golden. Serve warm.

Makes 4 to 6 servings

mini brownie cups

¼ cup (½ stick) light margarine
2 egg whites
1 egg
¾ cup sugar
⅔ cup all-purpose flour
⅓ cup HERSHEY'S Cocoa
½ teaspoon baking powder
¼ teaspoon salt
  Mocha Glaze (recipe follows)

1. Heat oven to 350°F. Line small muffin cups (1¾ inches in diameter) with paper baking cups or spray with vegetable cooking spray.

2. Melt margarine in small saucepan over low heat; cool slightly. Beat egg whites and egg in small bowl with electric mixer on medium speed until foamy; gradually add sugar, beating until slightly thickened and light in color. Stir together flour, cocoa, baking powder and salt; gradually add to egg mixture, beating until blended. Gradually add melted margarine, beating just until blended. Fill muffin cups ⅔ full with batter.

3. Bake 15 to 18 minutes or until wooden pick inserted in center comes out clean. Remove from pan to wire rack. Cool completely. Prepare Mocha Glaze; drizzle over tops of brownie cups. Let stand until glaze is set.

Makes 24 brownie cups

mocha glaze

¼ cup powdered sugar
¾ teaspoon HERSHEY'S Cocoa
¼ teaspoon powdered instant coffee
2 teaspoons hot water
¼ teaspoon vanilla extract

1. Stir together powdered sugar and cocoa in small bowl. Dissolve coffee in water; gradually add to sugar mixture, stirring until well blended. Stir in vanilla.

perfect peanut butter pudding

  2 cups milk
  2 eggs
  ⅓ cup creamy peanut butter
  ¼ cup packed brown sugar
  ¼ teaspoon vanilla
  ¾ cup shaved chocolate or shredded coconut (optional)

1. Preheat oven to 350°F. Grease 6 (3-ounce) ovenproof custard cups.

2. Combine milk, eggs, peanut butter, brown sugar and vanilla in blender; blend at high speed 1 minute. Pour into prepared custard cups. Place cups in 13×9-inch baking dish; carefully add enough hot water to baking dish to come halfway up sides of custard cups.

3. Bake 50 minutes or until pudding is set. Remove custard cups from pan; cool to room temperature. Refrigerate until ready to serve.

4. Just before serving, top each pudding with about 2 tablespoons shaved chocolate or shredded coconut, if desired.

Makes 6 servings

tip | Delicate foods, such as custards and soufflés, are sometimes baked in hot water baths. The baking dish is placed in a larger container that is filled halfway with hot, often boiling, water. During baking, the hot water bath provides a constant, steady heat source to the food, ensuring it will cook evenly without breaking or curdling.

peach-ginger crumble

   1 pound frozen sliced peaches, thawed
   2 very ripe pears, sliced (about 6 ounces)
  ¾ cup dried apricots, cut into ¼-inch pieces
   4 tablespoons packed dark brown sugar, divided
   1 tablespoon cornstarch
   1 teaspoon vanilla
 12 gingersnaps
   1 tablespoon canola or vegetable oil
  ½ teaspoon ground cinnamon

1. Preheat oven to 350°F. Spray 9-inch deep-dish pie pan with nonstick cooking spray.

2. Combine peaches, pears, apricots, 2 tablespoons brown sugar, cornstarch and vanilla in large bowl. Toss gently until well blended. Place in prepared pie pan.

3. Place gingersnaps in resealable food storage bag. Crush cookies with rolling pin to form coarse crumbs. Combine crumbs, remaining 2 tablespoons brown sugar, oil and cinnamon; mix well. Sprinkle evenly over fruit.

4. Bake 30 minutes or until fruit is bubbly. Cool 10 minutes on wire rack.   *Makes 6 servings*

The publisher would like to thank the companies and organizations listed below for the use of their recipes and photographs in this publication.

ACH Food Companies, Inc.

Bob Evans®

EAGLE BRAND®

Filippo Berio® Olive Oil

The Hershey Company

Nestlé USA

Ortega®, A Division of B&G Foods, Inc.

Sargento® Foods Inc.

Reprinted with permission of Sunkist Growers, Inc.
All Rights Reserved.

Unilever

acknowledgments

index

index

index

VOLUME MEASUREMENTS (dry)

$^1/_8$ teaspoon = 0.5 mL
$^1/_4$ teaspoon = 1 mL
$^1/_2$ teaspoon = 2 mL
$^3/_4$ teaspoon = 4 mL
1 teaspoon = 5 mL
1 tablespoon = 15 mL
2 tablespoons = 30 mL
$^1/_4$ cup = 60 mL
$^1/_3$ cup = 75 mL
$^1/_2$ cup = 125 mL
$^2/_3$ cup = 150 mL
$^3/_4$ cup = 175 mL
1 cup = 250 mL
2 cups = 1 pint = 500 mL
3 cups = 750 mL
4 cups = 1 quart = 1 L

VOLUME MEASUREMENTS (fluid)

1 fluid ounce (2 tablespoons) = 30 mL
4 fluid ounces ($^1/_2$ cup) = 125 mL
8 fluid ounces (1 cup) = 250 mL
12 fluid ounces (1$^1/_2$ cups) = 375 mL
16 fluid ounces (2 cups) = 500 mL

WEIGHTS (mass)

$^1/_2$ ounce = 15 g
1 ounce = 30 g
3 ounces = 90 g
4 ounces = 120 g
8 ounces = 225 g
10 ounces = 285 g
12 ounces = 360 g
16 ounces = 1 pound = 450 g

DIMENSIONS

$^1/_{16}$ inch = 2 mm
$^1/_8$ inch = 3 mm
$^1/_4$ inch = 6 mm
$^1/_2$ inch = 1.5 cm
$^3/_4$ inch = 2 cm
1 inch = 2.5 cm

OVEN TEMPERATURES

250°F = 120°C
275°F = 140°C
300°F = 150°C
325°F = 160°C
350°F = 180°C
375°F = 190°C
400°F = 200°C
425°F = 220°C
450°F = 230°C

BAKING PAN SIZES

Utensil	Size in Inches/Quarts	Metric Volume	Size in Centimeters
Baking or	8×8×2	2 L	20×20×5
Cake Pan	9×9×2	2.5 L	23×23×5
(square or	12×8×2	3 L	30×20×5
rectangular)	13×9×2	3.5 L	33×23×5
Loaf Pan	8×4×3	1.5 L	20×10×7
	9×5×3	2 L	23×13×7
Round Layer	8×1½	1.2 L	20×4
Cake Pan	9×1½	1.5 L	23×4
Pie Plate	8×1¼	750 mL	20×3
	9×1¼	1 L	23×3
Baking Dish	1 quart	1 L	—
or Casserole	1½ quart	1.5 L	—
	2 quart	2 L	—

metric conversion chart

160